Orchid Growing *for* Wimps

Orchid Growing *for* Wimps

TECHNIQUES FOR

THE "WISH I COULD

DO THAT" GARDENER

Ellen Zachos

Sterling Publishing Co., Inc.
New York

Book design by Richard Oriolo
Photography by Ellen Zachos
Chapter opener photography by Michael Hnatov Photography

Library of Congress Cataloging-in-Publication Data Available

10 9 8 7 6 5 4 3 2

Published by Sterling Publishing Company, Inc.
387 Park Avenue South, New York, N.Y. 10016
© 2002 by Ellen Zachos
Distributed in Canada by Sterling Publishing
$^{c}/o$ Canadian Manda Group, One Atlantic Avenue, Suite 105
Toronto, Ontario, Canada M6K 3E7
Distributed in Great Britain and Europe by Chrysalis Books
64 Brewery Road, London N7 9NT, England
Distributed in Australia by Capricorn Link (Australia) Pty. Ltd.
P.O. Box 704, Windsor, NSW 2756 Australia
Printed in China
All rights reserved

Sterling ISBN 0-8069-7935-6

This book is dedicated to my aunt, Victoria Zachos,

who has shared many things with me,

including her love of orchids.

Acknowledgments

I am enormously grateful to: Michael MacDonald, John Keane, and Elizabeth Zachos, for their willingness to repeatedly read this manuscript and their diplomatic delivery of constructive criticism; to Mark Hardy, Jane Gil, and my family for unflagging confidence and encouragement; to the Kahn family and the Bendheim family for allowing me to experiment and photograph in their greenhouses. This personal and practical support has been priceless. Special thanks to Mark Rose of Breckenridge Orchids, whose generosity and vast knowledge of all things orchid were invaluable to this project.

Rynchostyllos gigantea

Contents

CONTENTS

Angraecum hybrid

Ascocenda Carolina Skies

Orchid Growing *for* Wimps

Introduction

Welcome to the wonderful world of orchids; I'm so glad you could come. First, let me say that a true wimp wouldn't bother to read this book. A genuine wimp would simply let his or her orchid fade gradually into oblivion, barely noticing that what once was ravishing is now dead.

That's not you. You may not know a lot about orchids now, but you will. You're eager to learn, hungry for knowledge, ready to break out the bark mix and cork slabs and . . . but wait, I'm getting ahead of myself.

Did you receive an orchid as a gift, and now you wonder how to keep it alive? Maybe you bought yourself an orchid at your local home improvement store because it was gorgeous and such a good deal, and now you'd really like to get it to bloom again. Or maybe you've been growing houseplants for years and are ready to push the edge of your gardening envelope. Whatever your reasons may be, this book can help.

First you'll get a little background on orchids in general: how they grow in nature, and what this tells you about how to grow them best in your home. Then we'll go over basic care and the tools you'll need to provide it, including tips on potting media, special pots and bark mounts, and how to water and feed your orchids.

Next, we'll focus on sixteen different kinds of orchids, all of them com-

mercially available and easy to grow in a home environment. You'll get information on light, temperature, and water requirements, as well as facts about bloom habits and fragrance. You'll learn how to repot your orchids and how to keep them free of pests and diseases. I'll also point out several types of orchid that are not recommended for the beginning grower. (If I can help you avoid the pain of watching a loved one suffer, so much the better.)

For those of you who want to flex your gardening muscles, we'll discuss how to boost bloom with artificial lights and how to divide and multiply your orchids. By this point you'll be completely hooked, and you'll want—no you'll need—information on where to get more orchids and how to commune with fellow orchid lovers. This book gives you all this, and more.

Finally, there's a section on frequently asked questions, and a glossary that includes all the terms you'll see in **bold print** on their first appearance in the text of this book. This may sound like a lot, but actually, growing orchids isn't hard. I just want you to have the information you'll need to do it right. Knowledge is power.

So welcome to the wonderful world of orchids, "Wimps." Turn the page.

This grape-scented *Vanda* species grows as an epiphyte in Hawaii.

Not all orchids are temperamental tropicals. In fact, many make easy-going houseplants, requiring no more attention than the ubiquitous African violet. Maybe the mere idea of growing something as exotic as an orchid is intimidating, in which case, getting to know how these plants grow in nature is a good first step toward conquering your fear. You want to choose the right plant for your specific conditions in order to give yourself every opportunity for success. Knowing where your orchid came from will tell you what it needs in terms of light, temperature, drainage, and nutrition. Armed with this information, you can decide whether or not a specific orchid is right for your home.

Orchids are native to every continent on Earth except Antarctica. They grow on rocks, on trees, and in the ground. There are temperate orchids and tropical orchids, orchids that grow all year round, and orchids that require a dormant period.

Chapter 1

Not All Orchids Are Temperamental

(LEFT): *Vanilla planifolia* is the only "edible" orchid. Its seed pods are our vanilla beans. (RIGHT): *Dendrobium fimbriatum* v. oculatum

The orchid family is the largest plant family in the world, and it includes more than 20,000 different species. You'll usually see orchids tagged with two-part Latin names. The first part is the **genus** and the second denotes the **species**. A single genus can contain many species, and the species within a genus all share certain characteristics. A **hybrid** is a cross between two different species and can be manmade or occur naturally.

Most of the orchids we grow indoors are tropical orchids. Their forebears were natives of tropical rain forests and the jungles of South America, Africa, Asia,

and the South Pacific. Any rain forest has much more humid air than the average home or apartment, so this gives you a big clue: every orchid in this book will benefit from elevated humidity.

To put things in perspective, the average home or apartment in the U.S. has a humidity level of about 25% in winter. The average rain forest has a humidity level of greater than 90%. Now, obviously, 90% humidity in the home would be a very bad thing. You'd have mold in your carpets and fungus in your upholstery. However, a small boost in humidity will improve the health of both

GENUS, SPECIES, HYBRID, ETC.

Every orchid name is composed of a genus, plus either a species or hybrid name. If the orchid is unique, it may be given a cultivar name to distinguish it from other orchids of the same species or hybrid.

Genus	species	Hybrid	'Cultivar'
a group of plants classified together due to common ancestry; can be manmade or naturally occurring	a further division of a a genus; a closely related group of plants	offspring resulting from crossing two species	a single genetic representation of a species or hybrid
always capitalized; either italicized or underlined	not capitalized; either italicized or underlined	always capitalized; not italicized or underlined	set off in single quotation marks
Ludisia	*discolor*		'Negra'
Potinara		Hoku Gem	'Super Spots'

(TOP LEFT): **Take a large, empty saucer to make a drywell.** (BOTTOM LEFT): **Fill the bottom of the saucer with pebbles.** (ABOVE): **Pour water up to the top of the pebbles.** (BELOW): **Place your orchids on the wet pebbles. As water evaporates from the drywell, ambient humidity is raised around the plants.**

plants and people. In fact, even your wood furniture will appreciate a humidity level of about 40%, which is not difficult to achieve.

Perhaps you already have a humidifier sitting in the closet that you haul out when someone has a cold. Well, haul it out now and set it up near your orchid. Maybe you have a few other houseplants scattered throughout your apartment. If they share the same light and temperature requirements as your orchid, group them together. As the plants **transpire** the level of humidity surrounding them increases, and all the plants benefit.

The easiest way to increase the humidity around any plant is to create a **drywell**. If your plant has a saucer under it, you're halfway there, and if it doesn't then you're going to have a dripping mess on your hands as soon as you water it. So get a saucer fast. Choose a saucer slightly larger than the diameter of the top of your pot. If your orchid is in a six-inch pot, try an eight- or ten-inch saucer, depending on the space you have available. Fill the saucer with gravel to about ¼ inch below the rim, and pour water over the pebbles until it just covers the top of the stones.

Sit your orchid on the wet gravel. As the water evaporates from around the pebbles it increases the humidity of the air closely surrounding the plant. If the water level is too high and the bottom of the orchid pot sits in

(TOP AND BOTTOM LEFT): **A thick, absorbent layer of white velamen surrounds the green roots of this orchid.** (ABOVE): **Velamen roots and a keiki sprout from the stem of this** *Dendrobium*.

water, root rot could develop. So, be careful not to let this happen. You can also use trays or cookie sheets filled with gravel to create larger drywells that accommodate groups of plants in a single location, like a large bay window or a tabletop. If you remember to fill your drywell whenever the water level drops, your orchids will be very happy.

In their native habitats, most tropical orchids are **epiphytes**: plants that live on tree trunks and branches rather than on the ground. Special aerial roots, called **velamen** roots, anchor orchids to trees but do not take any nutrients from the host. Epiphytes are not parasites.

Their roots absorb moisture from the surrounding humid air, and they get their nutrients from debris that falls into the plants from the **canopy** above.

Epiphyte roots are constantly exposed to the air, and the entire plant benefits from the excellent air circulation that comes with perching high above the ground. So how do we satisfy these requirements when growing an epiphytic orchid in the home? Most houseplants are potted in soil, or a **soilless mix** that looks like soil but is lighter-weight. This type of potting mix closely surrounds a plant's roots, providing it with anchorage, oxygen, water, and nutrition. An epiphyte also needs all of these things, but grows better if its roots are not completely surrounded and have increased contact with the air. So, instead of a traditional potting mix, use a coarser medium, such as **bark chips** or **tree fern fiber**. These substances provide anchorage yet allow contact between the plant's roots and the surrounding air.

In nature, an epiphyte gets the moisture it requires from rainfall and from the humid air typical of the tropical rain forest. Its super-absorbent velamen roots soak up moisture quickly, and since they grow exposed to the air, they dry off quickly, too. If the roots of an epiphyte are kept constantly wet, they will rot and the plant will die; the roots need to dry out between waterings. A coarse medium, like bark chips, is quick-draining and does not hold moisture for too long against the roots, so it would be a good choice. Soil, or a soilless mix, retains moisture longer and can encourage root rot in epiphytes. It is not the best potting medium for most orchids.

Some epiphytic orchids grow best mounted on pieces of cork, tree fern fiber, or branches that you can hang from hooks as you would a hanging basket. An orchid mount-

(LEFT): **bark mix** (RIGHT): **a bark mounted** *Potinara* **Hoku Gem 'Super Spots'**

CONTAINERS

While many orchids can grow well in several different types of containers, the following chart shows you the optimum container choices for each species.

Orchids for Wimps	Plastic	Clay	Wooden Box	Slab Mounted
Phalaenopsis	X	X		
Paphiopedilum	X	X		
Brassavola nodosa		X	X	X
Dendrobium		X		
Oncidium		X		
Cattleya		X	X	
Cattleya Alliance		X	X	X
Dendrochilum magnum		X	X	
Phragmipedium	X			
Ludisia & other jewel orchids	X	X		
Miltonia	X	X		
Encyclia cochleata		X		
Brassia		X	X	
Doritis pulcherrima	X	X		
Cochleanthes amazonica	X	X		
Gongora quinquenervis		X		

ed in this way will require more frequent watering than an orchid in a pot, but its care is not more complicated, just more frequent.

A few of the orchids recommended in this book are **terrestrial** orchids, and these require a different kind of potting medium. Terrestrial orchids grow best in a finer, more water-retentive mix. However, this does not mean you should use a heavy soil. Many orchids that grow on the floor of the rain forest do not actually grow in soil. Rather, their roots grow through patches of moss and **humus**, which are lighter-weight than soil but still retain adequate moisture to support the plant. Humus is decomposing organic matter. It can include leaf mold, small pieces of bark, animal waste, or dead

four types of fertilizer

This *Phalaenopsis* has a monopodial growth habit.

insects. Commercial mixes containing humus are also available.

In general, orchids are not heavy feeders. Use a balanced liquid fertilizer at half the recommended strength every other week during the growing season. A **balanced fertilizer** contains equal amounts of nitrogen, phosphates, and potassium, and it encourages good all-around growth. The bottle is marked with three equal numbers, e.g., 5-5-5 or 10-10-10, which indicate the percentage of the fertilizer made up of each nutrient. Nitrogen specifically promotes healthy, green foliage; phosphates are for good flower and fruit production; and potassium assists with root development.

Some orchids may have special nutritional needs. For example, an orchid mounted on bark will require more nitrogen, since it is not surrounded by a slowly decom-

posing potting mix. In this case, give your orchid a **foliar feed** with a fertilizer that has a higher first number, e.g., 30-10-10. If your orchid isn't blooming when it should, try feeding it with a **bloom booster**, i.e., a fertilizer with a higher middle number, such as 5-10-5.

All orchids can be categorized as having one of two growth habits:

1. Some, like *Phalaenopsis,* grow from a single point and have a vertical growth habit (**monopodial orchids**). In nature they grow upward, climbing up a tree trunk with the help of their roots.

2. Others, like *Cattleyas,* grow from a **rhizome** that runs underground (**sympodial orchids**). Vertical growths rise from the underground stem, with each new growth originating from the base of the plant, in front of the last upright growth.

This *Sophrolaeliocattleya* has a sympodial growth habit.

When you know where your orchid grows in nature, you also learn something about the kind of light it requires. Terrestrial orchids need less light than epiphytic orchids. This makes sense when you recall that they flourish on the forest floor, which is considerably shadier than up among the branches. In your home, a terrestrial orchid will grow well in an eastern window, or even in a bright, unobstructed northern window.

Although epiphytes receive more light than terrestrials, most do not receive direct sunlight. The leaves of their host trees shade them from the hot sun, providing a dappled light best reproduced in the home by an unobstructed eastern window or a southern or western win-

dow with a sheer curtain. Epiphytic orchids with higher light requirements grow higher in the forest canopy and receive more direct sunlight. These orchids can safely tolerate full light in a southern or western window.

There are many orchids that grow best within specific temperature ranges, some of which are not easy to reproduce in the home. (Orchids native to the cloud forests of the upper Andes mountains like it a little colder than we do!) However, since so many commercially available orchids prefer average household temperatures, temperature should not seriously limit your plant choices. In general, our homes are cooler in winter than in summer, and cooler at night than dur-

TEMPERATURE RANGES

Many orchids will bloom better with a nighttime temperature drop of about ten degrees (F), which frequently occurs naturally in a large bay window. Even orchids that don't require a temperature drop will tolerate somewhat cooler temperatures at night, but don't let your orchids get below 55°F.

Orchids for Wimps	Normal Household Temperatures	Cooler at Night	Keep Below 80°F
Phalaenopsis	X	X	
Paphiopedilum	X	X	
Brassavola nodosa	X		
Dendrobium	X		
Oncidium	X		
Cattleya	X	X	
Cattleya Alliance	X	X	
Dendrochilum magnum	X		
Phragmipedium	X		
Ludisia & other jewel orchids	X		
Miltonia	X	X	X
Encyclia cochleata	X	X	
Brassia	X	X	
Doritis pulcherrima	X		
Cochleanthes amazonica	X		
Gongora quinquenervis	X		

ing the day, and this is just how most orchids like it. In some instances, bloom is triggered by a drop in temperature, and this will occur naturally as the seasons change. If you're growing an orchid that requires a cooler nighttime temperature than you find comfortable, move it to a windowsill. Temperatures here can be ten degrees Fahrenheit lower than at the center of the room. Just be sure not to let the foliage touch the window glass, or the cold could damage the plant tissue.

Obviously, it's important to know what kind of orchid you have before you can know how to care for it. A terrestrial orchid mounted on a piece of cork will not survive for long, just as an epiphyte potted in heavy garden soil is bound to rot quickly. If you know the natural growth habits of your orchid, you can do your best to duplicate these conditions in your home.

You've brought your new orchid home, and now you have to take care of it. First, look at how your orchid is potted, and, taking into consideration the needs of your specific plant, ask yourself if it's planted in the right kind of material. Do you have a moisture loving terrestrial mounted on cork bark or a drought-tolerant epiphyte potted in soil? Probably not, but if so, you'll need to repot it right away. This chapter covers the basics of potting mixes, containers, and how to mount your orchid on a slab of bark or tree fern fiber.

Potting Mixes

You've certainly noticed by now that your orchid didn't come potted in soil, as so many other houseplants do. Most orchids are planted in a coarse, quick-draining mix consisting of pine bark, tree fern

tree fern fiber

Chapter 2

General Care

and

Paraphernalia

MIX INGREDIENTS

pine bark

Different-size pieces of pine bark are the most popular potting materials for orchids. Pine bark is easy to work with, inexpensive, and provides excellent root aeration. It does not provide much nutrition, and orchids potted in bark should be fed regularly.

tree fern fiber

Tree fern fiber decomposes slowly and provides excellent root aeration. However, it does not retain a lot of water, making it more suitable for orchid growers living in areas of high humidity (like Florida and Hawaii).

perlite

Perlite is a processed volcanic material. It is sterile, decomposes slowly, and has excellent water-retention ability.

sphagnum moss

A spongy plant material harvested from bogs, sphagnum moss is antiseptic and can hold ten times its weight in water.

peat moss

Dead sphagnum moss decomposes to form peat moss. It retains large amounts of water, and is a much finer-grade potting material than live sphagnum moss.

charcoal

(hardwood charcoal, not pressed powder briquettes) Horticultural charcoal is antiseptic and neutralizes dangerous bacteria in the potting medium. It also absorbs the acids produced by decomposing bark mixes and is sometimes said to "sweeten" the mix.

(LEFT): **horticultural charcoal**

(RIGHT TOP): **perlite** (RIGHT MIDDLE): **sphagnum moss** (RIGHT BOTTOM): **peat moss**

fiber, **perlite, sphagnum moss, peat moss**, or a mixture of the above. These mixes have lots of space between their particles and provide just the right amount of contact between orchid roots and the air. They also hold the right amount of moisture for these epiphytic plants.

You can buy bags of prepared orchid mix at most home improvement stores, as well as at garden centers and plant stores. These mixes are generally well-prepared, and I use them all the time. But, if you feel ambitious, perhaps you'd like to create your own orchid mix. The type of orchid you're working with will determine which base material you should use. An epiphyte requires a more quickly draining mix than a terrestrial orchid. An especially drought-tolerant epiphyte should be grown in a bark mix composed of larger pieces. A terrestrial orchid can also be potted in bark, but the nuggets should be small and the bark should be mixed with other, finer grained materials.

Most orchid mixes are composed primarily of bark or tree fern fiber, with the balance of the mix made up of varying amounts of the other materials described in the sidebar. Bark is simpler to work with than tree fern fiber; it's easier to fit in around the orchid's roots, it does not require preliminary soaking, and it's less expensive. Therefore, I recommend the beginner experiment with bark-based potting mixes first. The following are three basic recipes:

terrestrial orchid mix
- 2 parts fine grade fir bark (⅛ - ¼ inch pieces)
- 6 parts peat moss
- 1 part **horticultural charcoal**
- 1 part perlite

general epiphyte mix
- 5 parts medium grade fir bark (¼ - ½ inch pieces)
- 2 parts peat moss
- 1 part horticultural charcoal
- 2 parts perlite

drought-tolerant epiphyte mix
- 5 parts large grade fir bark (½ - 1 inch pieces)
- 2 parts sphagnum moss
- 1 part horticultural charcoal
- 2 parts perlite

Special Orchid Containers

Many orchids are potted in boxes made from wooden slats or in clay pots with extra holes and slits in the bottom and sides. These containers allow more air to reach the roots of the orchids than a plastic pot or a clay pot with a single drainage hole. Most orchid roots require excellent **aeration** to grow well. If the roots stay wet and soggy, the plant will rot and die.

Plants in non-porous containers, such as plastic or metal, dry out more slowly than plants in containers made from porous materials, such as wood or unglazed clay. A pot made from a porous material will lose water through

orchid pots and box

evaporation through the container walls, as well as through the soil surface. Containers made from non-porous materials will lose water only from the soil surface. This means that the potting mix in a clay or wooden pot will dry out more quickly and provide better aeration for the orchid's roots. Beginning growers frequently overwater, and if their orchids are potted in plastic, this could be fatal. If you're just starting out and you worry that you may unwittingly overwater, grow your orchid in a porous pot.

Bark Mounts

All epiphytes can be grown mounted on tree fern fiber, **cork**, or wood. Remember, in nature they grow perched in trees. Since orchids are adaptable creatures and growing them in pots is easier, most home growers plant orchids in containers. Still, there are some orchids that thrive only when mounted. Caring for orchids displayed

in this manner is no more complicated than caring for orchids potted in traditional pots; mounted orchids simply require more frequent watering and feeding. Mounting the orchid is quite simple, and it's an enjoyable project for anyone who likes crafts.

Choose your mounting material based on aesthetics and the moisture needs of your plant (see sidebar). You'll need the following additional materials:

- a hot glue gun with a low temperature setting
- glue sticks
- ten- or twelve-gauge stainless steel wire
- monofilament fishing line
- sphagnum moss
- one inch "U" staples

tree fern fiber, cork, and wood mounts

This potted orchid can be mounted on cork with hot glue.

ORCHID MOUNTS

tree fern fiber
Slabs of tree fern fiber retain more moisture than wood or cork.

cork slabs
Cork slabs stay the driest of these three materials.

wood
A hardwood such as cypress or sassafras is the longest lasting mount material.

Brassavola cordosa

Cork Slab

1. Fasten a "U" staple to the top of your cork slab. You should be able to gently tap it into place with a hammer. This will be your hanger once the orchid is mounted.

2. Lay the cork piece flat, and find a place on the cork where the orchid fits well. The surface of the cork is ridged and grooved, and your orchid will fit best into a hollow.

3. Mark the spots where the orchid and cork will touch. You'll only need two or three contact points.

4. Using your glue gun on the low setting, dab glue onto the cork. Be aware that on the high setting the melted glue can damage plant tissue. The glue dries quickly, so have everything laid out and ready to go.

5. Press the orchid gently onto the cork, making sure each contact point is met. Allow the glue to dry for an hour or two.

6. When the glue has dried, soak the entire slab for ten to fifteen minutes, then allow any extra water to drain before hanging your orchid in place.

7. After a few months, check your orchid's roots. They will have grown into the cork, holding the orchid firmly in place.

Tree Fern Fiber

1. Fasten a "U" staple to the top of your tree fern fiber slab. (You may be able to push this between the fibers manually or you may need to use a small hammer.) This will be your hanger once the orchid is mounted. For extra security, add a bead of glue to each side of the "U" staple to secure it in place.

2. Lay the slab flat and place a small clump of sphagnum moss in the center. The clump should be about the same size as the root system of the plant you are mounting. It will help retain moisture and protect the roots.

3. Place the orchid on top of the moss. Center the plant so roots have room to grow downward and the plant has room to grow up.

4. Place another small clump of sphagnum moss on top of the root system. The entire root system does *not* have to be covered.

5. Cut a twelve-inch piece of stainless steel wire and bend it into a U-shape. Place the "U" over the moss/root mass and gently push it into the tree fern fiber. (The second layer of sphagnum moss will protect roots from being cut by the wire.)

6. Twist the wire in back, making it tight enough to hold the orchid in place, but not so tight as to damage the plant. Clip the ends and tuck them into the bark.

7. Soak the entire slab for ten to fifteen minutes, then allow any extra water to drain before hanging your orchid in place.

8. After a few months, check your orchid roots. They will have grown into the tree fern fiber, firmly anchoring your plant in place.

Wood

1. Fasten a hanger to the top of your wood slab. You can either hammer a "U" staple into the top of your piece of wood or drill a hole through the wood and tie a loop of five-pound test monofilament.

2. Remove your orchid from its pot and tease the bark chips from between its roots. Now it's ready to be mounted.

3. Lay the wood flat and place a small clump of sphagnum moss in the center. The clump should be about the same size as the root system of the plant you are mounting. This will help retain moisture and protect the roots.

4. Place the orchid on top of the moss. Center the orchid/moss so roots have room to grow downward and the plant has room to grow up.

5. Place another small clump of sphagnum moss on top of the root system. The entire root system does not have to be covered.

6. Using clear monofilament, tie the orchid to the wood, wrapping the plant several times. Fasten the plant firmly, but not so tightly that the filament cuts into any plant tissue. (The second layer of sphagnum moss protects roots from being cut by the filament.)

7. Soak the entire slab for ten to fifteen minutes, then allow any extra water to drain before hanging your orchid in place.

8. After a few months, check your orchid roots. They will have grown onto the wood slab, and you can cut and remove the monofilament.

Even if your orchid can grow perfectly well in a pot, you might want to try mounting it on wood or bark just for the fun of it. An orchid growing this way will need more frequent watering than an orchid in a pot. Their roots are exposed to the air (since there is no potting medium surrounding them) and therefore they dry out more quickly. You'll probably need to water every other day, and the easiest way to do this is to soak the whole piece in a pan of water for five or ten minutes. It's also a good idea to mist mounted orchids once or twice a day. Yes, this is slightly more work than caring for a potted orchid, but it looks great, and you'll feel like a pro!

Your orchid is now perfectly potted in the appropriate container or mounted on a suitable slab. The next step is to establish a feeding and watering schedule that both you and your plant can live with.

Watering Basics

Plants don't want little sips of water here and there; they like a long, satisfying drink. Every time you water your orchid, do so until excess water runs out the drainage holes of the plant's container. If you water a plant incompletely, you encourage root growth only in the portion of potting mix that has been watered. By watering thoroughly, you promote deep root growth throughout the pot.

Since many orchids are grown in slatted boxes or pots with extra drainage holes, water drains from the containers very quickly. Even orchids in regular pots drain quickly if potted in an appropriate, porous mix. If you suspect your orchid needs more moisture (e.g., if

Chapter 3

Watering, Feeding, Misting

(TOP LEFT): **This small orchid pot can be submerged for thorough watering.** (TOP RIGHT): **Choose a bowl that will hold your orchid pot.** (BOTTOM LEFT): **Fill the bowl with water up to the top of the orchid pot's rim.**

the leaves or **pseudobulbs** look shriveled, if new leaves emerge looking folded or pleated), give them a good soak. Choose a pot or pan slightly larger than your orchid container and fill it with tepid water. Place the orchid container in the pot of water and let it soak for ten to fifteen minutes. Remove it from the pot, let it drain in a sink or tub, then put it back in position. This kind of TLC will help your orchid thrive. Not only does the medium get fully soaked, but the leaves and stems of the plant are cleaned simultaneously, allowing them to breathe and grow better.

Most orchids respond well to misting with water from a pump bottle. Thicker-leafed orchids (like *Phalaenopsis* and *Cattleyas*) are less demanding of high humidity, so if daily misting is more than you can manage, start with one of these. It's no crime to say, "I'll never spray my orchid once a day." The crime is in saying, "Yeah, I can do that," if it's not true. Know thyself, then choose thine orchid.

It is widely held that overwatering kills more orchids than underwatering. To the untrained eye, the results look the same. When plants are watered too infrequently, their roots don't absorb enough water and the plant shrivels and dies. When plants are watered too frequently their roots never dry out the way they should. As a result, they rot, and the plant has no way to absorb water or nutrients. Its leaves start to look shriveled, and the plant eventually dies.

Many orchids are epiphytes, and these especially need to dry out between waterings. Use the information on watering frequency included in each orchid profile as a starting point. If your home is particularly hot and dry, try watering one day sooner than recommended, i.e., every three days instead of every four. If your home is cool and humid, you can water one day later than recommended. Watch and observe your orchid. A problem caught in the early stages doesn't have to be fatal.

Feeding

Use a balanced liquid fertilizer at half the recommended strength every other week during the growing season. For most of us the growing season begins in early spring and continues through early fall. If you notice a new leaf

40

Let your orchid soak for ten to fifteen minutes.

starting, this is a good indication that the growing season has begun.

For a definition of a balanced fertilizer, see Chapter One.

Fertilizer can be added to water and given to your orchid when you water. Or, it can be mixed with water and sprayed onto the leaves with a mister. This is called a foliar feed. If you choose the latter, make sure you spray early in the day so any liquid left standing on the leaves has plenty of time to evaporate. Standing water at cooler nighttime temperatures is a breeding ground for plant diseases.

As a potting medium, pine bark does not provide a lot of nutrition, so even though orchids are not heavy feeders, they need regular fertilization. While time release plant foods are convenient and popular, they are not well-suited to orchid cultivation. These fertilizers come in granular and stick form. The stick form does not make good contact with bark mixes and therefore does not dissolve evenly. The granules can fall straight through the bark nuggets and also dissolve irregularly. It's best to stick with liquid or water-soluble fertilizers for orchids.

Occasionally, your orchid may need extra help from a bloom booster. It's not difficult to figure out when your orchid should flower again. Different types of orchids bloom with varying frequency and at different times of the year. (You'll find this information in the individual orchid profiles.) You probably acquired your orchid when it was in flower, so make a note of the date, and when you think it's time for your orchid to bloom again, watch carefully. If you spot a bud or a bloom spike, be sure not to let your orchid get too cold or dry, or the buds may die and fall off. If you don't see buds when you're expecting them, try feeding your orchid with a bloom booster. A month or two of fertilization with a plant food specially formulated to encourage bloom can help bring your orchid into flower.

There are many commercially available fertilizers intended specifically for orchids. You can choose from liquid or water soluble powders, organic or inorganic formulas. Regular houseplant fertilizers are also useful, and come in both balanced and bloom-boosting formulas.

Over-fertilization can be deadly, but fortunately it is not hard to detect. A white, crusty build-up on the edge of your pot or on the surface of the mix indicates that the fertilizer salts are not being fully **flushed** from the container. If this happens, repot your orchid in fresh potting mix, and adjust your feeding schedule. Too much fertilizer can burn the roots, which first results in foliage damage, and, eventually can kill the plant. With fertilization, it's better to err on the side of too little rather than too much.

Phalaenopsis

If you've received an orchid as a gift, there's an excellent chance it's a Phalaenopsis *(fail-uh-nóp-sis)*. Phalaenopsis *orchids are commonly known as moth orchids because their delicate, large flowers seem to hover on their bloom stalks like moths against a dark summer sky. They're some of the easiest orchids to grow in a typical home environment and they may bloom continuously for months at a time.*

**Phalaenopsis
Chromium
Emperor**

You probably got your Phalaenopsis *when it was in gloriously full bloom, and you'd like to keep it that way as long as possible. You'd also like it to bloom again and again.* Phalaenopsis *are the longest-blooming of the orchids commonly sold as houseplants. At the very least, your flowers should last two or three months; a coolish spot (around 65° F) will help prolong bloom time.*

Chapter 4

Individual
Orchid
Profiles

(TOP LEFT): *Phalaenopsis* **Chromium Emperor** (BOTTOM LEFT): *Phalaenopsis* **Mini Mark** x *Phalaenopsis* **Philippience** (TOP RIGHT): *Phalaenopsis* **Brother Bungor** (BOTTOM LEFT): *Phalaenopsis* **Golden Bells**

Greatest Characteristics

Each of the recommended orchids has numerous excellent qualitites, and is, of course, easy to grow. This chart highlights the most outstanding characteristic of each species.

Orchids for Wimps	Grow it because...
Phalaenopsis	numerous gorgeous blooms last up to nine months
Paphiopedilum	long-lasting ladyslipper orchid flowers in low light
Brassavola nodosa	multiple fragrant blossoms last more than a month
Dendrobium	flowers come in many colors and shapes and last for months
Oncidium	bloom spikes hold numerous flowers and many are wonderfully perfumed
Cattleya	huge, vibrant blossoms are often fragrant and come in many colors
Cattleya Alliance	wide range of colors, shapes, and sizes, many of which fit on your windowsill
Dendrochilum magnum	long chains of bloom have a strong citrusy scent
Phragmipedium	months of bloom and literally impossible to overwater
Ludisia & other jewel orchids	these low light orchids are beautiful even when they're not in bloom
Miltonia	large flowers available in many colors with detailed markings
Encyclia cochleata	uniquely shaped miniature orchid fits on a window sill
Brassia	numerous, large, exotic flowers are gently fragrant
Doritis pulcherrima	dainty flowers open in mid-summer
Cochleanthes amazonica	large fragrant flowers open several times a year with a spicy scent
Gongora quinquenervis	multiple pendant bloomstalks show off their flowers twice a year

This *Phalaenopsis* has had two older bloom stalks cut off and is blooming a third time from the same stem. Can you see where the nubs of the old stalks are?

When the last flower wilts and fades, cut the stalk just above the second **node** and wait a few weeks. Chances are good (about 60%) that you'll see a second bloom stalk branching off at an angle from your cut.

I gave my mother a Phal for Mother's Day and a month later she called to say the cat had knocked it off the windowsill and broken the flower stalk. She was so disappointed. I told her not to give up hope, and sure enough, five weeks later another entire spike of flowers was ready to open. That orchid bloomed non-stop for nine months; not bad for a twenty dollar investment from the local home improvement store.

Phalaenopsis are *not* fragile tropical beauties. In nature they grow in the **understory** of the rain forest (below the tops of tall trees) where they are protected from direct sun by tropical foliage. Phals are epiphytes and have developed specialized roots that hold them in place on tree branches. These roots (called velamen roots) are white and fleshy, and you may wonder why they're growing up, out of your potted plant, rather than down into the potting medium. They absorb water and nutrients from the surrounding humid air.

Many first-time growers mistakenly think these are bloom stalks. While the tips of the aerial roots may be greenish, the roots will mostly be white in color; in contrast, *Phalaenopsis* bloom stalks are greenish-purple. Some orchid beginners trim these roots or poke them down into the pot, not realizing that there are other roots in

the pot, anchoring the orchid in place. Leave the white, aerial roots as they are; it's the normal growth habit for the *Phalaenopsis*.

Consider the native habitat of the *Phalaenopsis* when caring for your orchid. They grow best in bright, indirect

Phalaenopsis with aerial roots growing up and out of the pot.

(LEFT): *Phalaenopsis* Muted Swan has variegated foliage. (RIGHT): *Phalaenopsis* foliage size comparison: *Phalaenopsis* Mini Mark vs. *Phalaenopsis* Gigantea 'Rocky Spots'

light (remember, the jungle understory), which is equivalent to the sunlight in an eastern window, or in a western or southern window with a sheer curtain. While the foliage may look healthy in a northern window, you probably won't get your Phal to reflower without artificial light to supplement the weaker, northern light. If the leaves of your plant turn yellowish, you may be giving your orchid too much light. Very dark green leaves are an indication of too little light.

The humidity level of the average household is far below that of the tropical rain forest, but fortunately, *Phalaenopsis* orchids are adaptable plants. They are also fairly drought-tolerant, and a plant in a six-inch pot can easily go five to seven days between waterings. Try creating a drywell for your orchid to give it a humidity boost. This consists of filling the saucer with gravel and adding water to the level of the top of the stones. The roots of the plant will be kept clear of the standing water, which, as it evaporates, raises the humidity around the plant.

Your orchid probably arrived potted in bark chips. Remember that the *Phalaenopsis* grows in trees and does best when its roots have contact with the air and don't stay soggy. Bark is a well-aerated, quick-draining potting medium; unlike traditional potting mix, it is difficult to overwater an orchid potted in bark. On the down side, bark provides very little nutrition for the plant, so be sure to feed your orchid regularly. Use a balanced fertilizer at half strength in spring and summer, then try a bloom booster in autumn. This, combined with the lower temperatures of fall, should induce the plant to bloom. In general, *Phalaenopsis* grow well at normal household temperatures. If you're feeling confident, try giving your Phal three weeks at about 60°F to guarantee a bumper crop of bloom. But be careful: below 55°F this orchid may drop its buds.

The number one cause of death among *Phalaenopsis* is too much or too little water. Too little water is indicated by shriveled leaves and shrunken, dry aerial roots. Too much water causes roots to rot. They are then unable to absorb water and nutrients, so the visual clues are similar to those caused by underwatering, as the plant becomes dehydrated. Start with a watering schedule of every four to five days in summer or every seven to eight days in winter, then adjust depending on your climate.

The second major cause of *Phalaenopsis* fatalities is **crown** rot. This results from water collecting in the crown of leaves, where it acts as a breeding ground for fungi. However, if you make sure to water early in the day, any water that accumulates between the leaves should evaporate fairly quickly in daylight. Evaporation slows significantly during darker, evening hours.

Phals are slow growers; you can expect to see two or three new leaves annually. They'll need repotting about once a year. Wait until your orchid has finished blooming to repot, and then do so only when the tips of the aerial roots are green. This indicates that the plant is in active growth. Phals typically bloom about once a year, so don't worry if it's been six months since you've seen a flower. Make a note of when your orchid last flowered, and look for a new bloom spike to start about ten months later.

Phalaenopsis are available with a wide range of flower colors, including white, pink, yellow, deep rose, and stripes, frequently with dramatically contrasting "**lips**." While some orchids aren't particularly attractive out of bloom, the *Phalaenopsis* has thick, straplike leaves that are pleasant to look at year round. There are **variegated** varieties, miniatures, and giant-leafed **cultivars**; in other words, there's a Phal to suit every taste.

Paphiopedilum

Paphiopedilum (paf-ee-oh-péh-dih-lum) orchids are mysterious and exotic, with flowers that appear almost to be carved from wax. Yet these tropical beauties easily adapt to the home environment. Their distinctive "lip" looks like a slipper, which is why they are commonly known as slipper orchids. Their striking blooms can last two or three months and come in many colors, including yellow, rose, green, white, and mahogany. They are striped and spotted, plump and curved, sensuous and exotic blooms.

Paphiopedilums can be divided into two groups, those with solid green leaves and those with mottled leaves. The green-leafed Paphs are considered cool-growing, and the mottled-leafed ones are considered warm-growing; however, both can be grown at normal household temperatures without complicated thermostat regulation.

Paphs are shade lovers in nature. Most are terrestrial orchids, but even though they grow on the ground, they don't grow in soil. Instead, they root in piles of humus and moss on the forest floor. Moss and humus hold moisture yet remain lightweight and provide good aeration for the orchid's roots.

As terrestrial orchids, Paphs require less light than their epiphytic relatives, which grow above them on tree trunks and branches. Paphs will tolerate morning rays but should be protected from the hotter afternoon sun.

Paphiopedilum **Brecho Garnet**

Paphiopedilum **Via Ojar**

Too much light will result in yellow foliage and hot sun can burn their leaves, leaving brown spots. Put your Paph in an eastern window, or if you must keep it in a southern or western window, be sure to protect it with a sheer curtain. Slipper orchids can also bloom in bright northern windows, making them particularly valuable to the home grower.

Unlike many orchids, *Paphiopedilums* do not have pseudobulbs that store moisture, nor do they have the thick, waxy **cuticle** typical of the *Phalaenopsis*, which slows the loss of water through the orchid leaves. Therefore it is particularly important that slipper orchids not be allowed to dry out. Remember, in nature they grow on the moist floor of tropical rain forests. Water your Paph when the top inch of the potting mix feels slightly moist and when the surface feels dry to the touch. This will probably be twice a week in summer, and once a week in winter, although you should adjust if you notice your plant showing signs of stress. All Paphs like high humidity, which you can easily supply by placing your plant on a drywell or grouping it with other houseplants.

Paphiopedilums require good aeration around their roots. A potting medium that is too heavy and/or wet will cause the roots to rot and the orchid to die. Keep in mind that while the orchids grow on the forest floor, their roots do not usually penetrate the soil, but grow through loosely textured moss and humus. In pot culture, this can best be approximated by **osmunda fiber**, sphagnum moss, fine bark chips (about 1/4" diameter), or a combination of one part perlite and two parts soil or soilless mix. *Paphiopedilums* are not suited to growth as bark-mounted specimens.

INDIVIDUAL ORCHID PROFILES

(TOP LEFT): *Paphiopedilum* **Greenvale** (BOTTOM LEFT): *Paphiopedilum*
Toll Booth (ABOVE): *Paphiopedilum* villosum

Paphiopedilums are not heavy feeders, in fact, they require less food than most other orchids. Give them a balanced fertilizer at half strength every three to four weeks. Paphs do not require frequent repotting, and can stay in the same pot for about two years. If the foliage starts to look wilted or yellowish, or if the potting mix breaks down and decays, it's time to repot. Wait until after the orchid has flowered, in order not to disturb the bloom.

Bacterial rot may occur if water is allowed to collect in the **leaf axils**. Symptoms of rot are black, mushy patches on leaves. These can quickly kill a plant. Water early in the day, so any remaining droplets have plenty of time to evaporate. If you must water in the evening, soak up any water left standing on the leaves.

If your Paph doesn't bloom, it may be the result of too little water, or improper exposure to light. If the leaves

(TOP): *Paphiopedilum* 'Janet Kenkle' Alba (BOTTOM): *Paphiopedilum Holdenii v. Album*

look puckered, wilted, or shriveled, try watering more frequently. If the foliage is yellowish, you may be giving your plant too much light. If the leaves are very dark green, you probably need to move your Paph to a slightly brighter spot.

While green-leafed and mottle-leafed Paphs can be grown successfully side by side, you may want to experiment with temperatures. Cool-growing Paphs generally prefer daytime temperatures of about 65°F and nighttime temperatures of about 55°F. This can easily be achieved by placing your orchid in a large bay window, or simply turning down the thermostat in the evening. Warm-growing Paphs grow and flower best with daytime temperatures ranging from 70°F to 80°F, and nighttime temperatures of about 65°F.

Paphiopedilum orchids are long-lasting, dependable bloomers, excellent choices for the beginning grower. Stake your plant as the bloom stalk lengthens, so the weight of the flower doesn't bend its stem. Once your Paph has opened, cooler temperatures (approximately 65°F) will prolong the bloom.

Slipper orchids come in a huge assortment of colors and sizes, and the variation of shapes and details is enormous. You could build an entire orchid collection of just Paphs. They are basically undemanding plants, and with a little attention to water and humidity, they will bloom faithfully, giving you years of satisfaction and exotic beauty.

Brassavola nodosa

Ah, the fragrant lady of the night! This is the common name for *Brassavola nodosa* (Brass-uh-vóle-ah no-dóe-sa), and as soon as you smell its complex, exotic perfume it will become one of your favorite orchids. This plant is a triple threat: it's very fragrant, it has beautiful flowers, and it's quite easy to grow.

There are many cultivars of *Brassavola nodosa*. Most are quite similar, varying slightly in the shape of their flowers. The blooms are delicate, with a heart-shaped white "lip" surrounded by spidery, greenish-yellow **tepals**. Bloom stalks hold one to three flowers among clumps of upright, almost cylindrical foliage. The smooth, thick leaves sit on top of inconspicuous pseudobulbs, which are about the same thickness as the leaves. Both the pseudobulbs and the leathery foliage make this orchid fairly drought-tolerant, so be sure not to overwater.

You've probably seen orchids planted in special slatted boxes, maybe on a visit to a botanic garden or in a greenhouse. Orchids planted in this manner require more frequent watering, so it's best to try it with a drought-tolerant specimen, like *Brassavola nodosa*. It's also an excellent way to ensure good root aeration and drainage, since the spaces between slats allow excess water to run off quickly and ensure that the root system will be exposed to the air. The boxes can either be hung or placed on a shelf, making this a particularly versatile way to grow your plant.

A *Brassavola nodosa* in a slatted box will probably need watering twice a week in summer and once every five to six days in winter. You can also grow this orchid in a traditional pot, or mounted on bark. In a pot, your plant will need water slightly less frequently, and mounted on bark it will require more frequent watering. *Brassavola* likes high light, so give it as much as you've got. A southern exposure is best, but your orchid will also bloom in strong western or eastern light. This is not a plant for a north-facing window.

If you have a yard, terrace, or balcony, consider hanging your *Brassavola* outside in summer. Although this orchid likes bright light indoors, it will need some shade outdoors. In their natural habitat, *Brassavolas* are epiphytes and are protected from the sun by the foliage of the trees they grow on. While it may not be immediately obvious, window glass greatly reduces the light intensity and spectrum of the sun's rays. A plant in full sun indoors

(ABOVE AND FACING PAGE): *Brassavola nodosa*

gets significantly less light than it would on just the other side of the window pane.

Brassavola nodosa grows best with higher humidity than most of us have at home. A drywell will help keep your plant in good shape. If you decide to hang your orchid, it would be impractical to create a drywell, so mist it once or twice a day as you walk past.

Brassavola nodosa's scent rivals that of the gardenia and is most fragrant in the evening. It also has another characteristic to recommend it: succession of bloom means this orchid can flower for months at a time. *Brassavola nodosa* commonly puts out one bunch of flowers after another, and this sequence is called succession of bloom. Each flower lasts for three or four weeks and a healthy specimen can have six to eight in bloom simultaneously. Not only are *Brassavola* orchids worth growing for their beauty and fragrance, but they are also frequently used to create extraordinary hybrids, several of which we'll discuss later. Like *Brassavola nodosa*, many of them make excellent houseplants.

Dendrobium Hybrids

The genus *Dendrobium* (den-dróh-bee-um) includes more than 1,000 different orchids, and many are easy to grow in the home. *Dendrobium* orchids bloom in sprays of three to fifteen flowers and can be breathtakingly gorgeous. They can bloom at any time of year, but most flower from early fall through January. Bloom stalks arch gracefully and may need to be staked if the flowers are numerous. *Dendrobium* flowers last from four to eight weeks and range in color from deep purple to white, yellow, and green.

Two kinds of *Dendrobium* are especially easy to grow in the home: the phalaenopsis *Dendrobium* and the antelope *Dendrobium*. The phalaenopsis *Dendrobiums* are so named because their flowers resemble those of the moth orchid. Antelope *Dendrobiums* get their name from their hornlike **petals** and **sepals**.

Both groups are tropical epiphytes and have basically the same care requirements. They grow best in high light, and indoors they'll take as much light as you can give them. However, a *Dendrobium* in a southern window may need a little shade in summer to keep the leaves from burning; a sheer curtain will do fine. If you'd like to move your orchid outside in summer, hang it from a tree or underneath something else that will give it dappled light.

Like most epiphytic orchids, *Dendrobiums* require excellent drainage; their roots absorb moisture quickly and in nature, where they grow hanging from trees, their roots dry off quickly, too. *Dendrobiums* will not tolerate a soggy potting medium; if their roots stay damp, the plants will rot and die. Use a clay pot for these orchids rather than

(ABOVE): *Dendrobium* **Lorrie Mortimer has the "horns" typical of the antelope** *Dendrobiums.*

(LEFT):
Dendrobium **Lim Lchong**

Dendrobium hybrid

plastic, which retains moisture longer. During the growing season (spring and summer), water your *Dendrobium* every two to three days. In winter, you can water once a week.

Dendrobiums have small root systems, and it's not unusual to see plants that are two feet tall in pots only six inches wide. These orchids bloom best when they're **root-bound**, so resist the temptation to overpot. If your *Dendrobium* is top-heavy and tips over, hang the pot from a hook, or stand the entire plant, including the pot, inside a larger pot to give it more weight at the base. Don't replant the orchid, since it can rot in a pot that's too large.

You'll only need to repot your *Dendrobium* once every two or three years. It's okay to let the aerial roots grow over the edge of the pot. When it's time to repot, remember that *Dendrobiums* are sensitive to transplanting. While many orchids can be repotted any time of year, it's best to repot *Dendrobiums* in spring. Afterwards, keep your orchid out of bright sun for two weeks to allow its roots to settle in, then move it back to its original position.

Dendrobiums are heavier feeders than many other orchids, so fertilize them every other week in spring and summer. At the beginning of autumn, stop feeding your *Dendrobium* and water it once a week until you see a bloom spike begin to form. Then increase your watering to twice a week. Once the flowers start to open, return to a once-a-week watering schedule.

Dendrobium orchids are some of the easiest orchids to **propagate,** because they readily form keikis. A **keiki** is an offset, a new orchid that grows out of the old, forming its own root system while still attached to the mother plant. When the roots are one to two inches long, cut off the stem just below the roots and plant the offset. You've just propagated your first orchid!

A keiki sprouts from the stem of this sympodial *Dendrobium* hybrid.

Oncidium

There are so many wonderful *Oncidium* (on-síh-dee-um) orchids available today that it's almost impossible to recommend just a few. *Oncidium* is a large genus, and within the group are plants of widely varying size, color, and fragrance. In fact, some *Oncidium* orchids are among the most irresistibly fragrant orchids there are.

Like *Dendrobiums*, *Oncidiums* are high light orchids and will thrive in a southern or western window. They'll also bloom in unobstructed eastern light. *Oncidiums* usually flower on long, branched stalks of delicate blooms that sway gently in a breeze, earning them the nickname "dancing ladies." The most common color combinations are yellow and brown, although pink, maroon, white, and orange are also available. *Oncidium* flowers can last up to two months and look particularly dramatic against a dark background, where their slim bloom stalk becomes invisible and the flowers appear to be suspended in midair.

Oncidiums are highly adaptable orchids and an excellent choice for the beginning grower who has plenty of light. Like *Dendrobiums*, the dancing lady grows best in a small pot, so it's not unusual to find a four-inch pot holding a plant with a flower stalk three feet tall. Its foliage is not as top-heavy as the *Dendrobium*, so tipping over shouldn't be a problem. However, the bloom spike may need to be staked if it is particularly long and crowded with flowers.

Oncidiums are epiphytes and are extremely drought-tolerant. Most have water storage tissue at the base of their

Oncidium 'Singh Gold'

Oncidium **'Sherry Baby' (sometimes spelled 'Shari Baby')**

leaves (pseudobulbs), which allows them to survive times of drought. This makes them lower maintenance than many other orchids, since they only need watering once every six to eight days. In a home environment, they grow best potted in clay, which dries out more quickly than plastic. Use a coarse, quick-draining mix of **pine bark nuggets** and let it dry out between waterings. Normal household temperatures and humidity are fine for the *Oncidiums* recommended here.

Sometimes you'll see the foliage of *Oncidium* orchids covered with a sprinkling of black spots. This is the result of water damage, caused by cold water being splashed on the leaves. While the spots don't usually harm the orchid, the damage can be unsightly, so try to be careful and avoid splatter.

The unscented yellow *Oncidiums* are beloved for their vibrant, saturated colors and the gentle movement of their flower stalks. The slightest breeze, or someone passing by, makes the plant sway like a beautifully suspended mobile.

Oncidium 'Sherry Baby' is one of the most fragrant *Oncidiums*, and it's easy to find at home improvement stores and garden centers. Its perfume can fill a room with a scent some call chocolaty and others swear reminds them of vanilla. Either way, it's a delicious perfume. The flowers are purple/maroon and pink with brown speckles. This orchid will bloom again and again in the home, given enough light.

Oncidium Twinkle 'Fragrance Fantasy'

Oncidium Twinkle 'Fragrance Fantasy' is an enchanting miniature that deserves a place on everyone's windowsill. A pot two inches in diameter holds a plant with eight-inch sprays of bloom, each producing twenty to thirty wonderfully sweet-scented flowers. The perfume is most fragrant during the day, and blooms last for at least a month.

Cattleya

If you close your eyes and say the word "orchid," the image that comes to mind is probably that of a *Cattleya* (Cat-láy-ah). You may not realize it, but if you ever gave or wore an orchid as a prom corsage, well, that's a *Cattleya*. It's a classic orchid and an excellent choice for beginners, because it's so easy to care for. *Cattleyas* come in a variety of rich colors, from brilliant whites to vibrant magentas and soft lavenders; some are also quite fragrant.

Cattleyas are epiphytes, and in nature they grow high in the rain forest canopy, just under the top layer of foliage. This tells you they are high-light plants, so give them a spot in a southern, western, or eastern window. *Cattleya* leaves can burn if they get too hot, so touch the foliage on a sunny day and if it feels hot (not warm, warm is okay), move your plant a little farther from the window or hang a sheer curtain to give it some protection from the heat.

For another clue on how *Cattleyas* grow best, look at their large pseudobulbs. These water-storage organs allow *Cattleyas* to survive the dry season in their native habitats; they are very drought-tolerant orchids. During the active growing season (spring and summer), water them twice a week. When the bloom is past, cut back on watering to once a week. If winter temperatures in your home are in the 65° to 70°F range, you may need to water your orchid only once every two weeks. However, if you notice the leaves looking shriveled, it's time to water.

No epiphytic orchid likes to be planted in a potting mix that stays soggy, and *Cattleyas* especially need to dry out between waterings. So never plant a *Cattleya* in regular houseplant potting mix; a quick-draining, medium-grade pine bark mix is a better choice for this orchid. This allows the velamen roots plenty of contact with the air and ensures that they'll dry out quickly, as they do in nature. Overwatering (i.e., watering too frequently) is a common cause of death among *Cattleyas*.

Cattleyas are less particular about humidity than many other orchids. While a drywell is always a good idea, *Cattleyas* will grow well with normal household humidity levels. However, if your home is particularly dry, for example, if you heat with a wood stove in winter, you should mist your leaves once a day. Don't spritz the flowers when they're open; too much moisture can cause fungus spots, and this isn't pretty.

The single most important element in getting *Cattleyas*

***Cattleya* pink hybrid**

to bloom is light intensity. If your plant has dark green leaves and they seem droopy, skinny, or weak, it's probably not getting enough light. *Cattleya* leaves should be a medium green and quite stiff and upright. Leaves that are yellow, look faded, or have brown scorch marks are getting too much light.

Cattleya orchids bloom best with cooler nighttime temperatures of 55° to 60°F, but if this is too difficult to accomplish, 65°F will be fine. Remember, the temperature next to your windowpane is definitely cooler than the temperature in the center of the room, so you may have this **microclimate** already built in.

Cattleyas are good-sized orchids and won't fit on a small windowsill. An orchid in a six-inch pot can be eighteen

Orchids

Cattleya pink hybrids at
Longwood Gardens,
Kennett Square, Pennsylvania

Cattleya **white hybrid**

inches tall and its foliage can spread to twelve inches wide. It may be a little top-heavy, so be careful it doesn't tip over. On the plus side, *Cattleya* flowers are also large and it's not unusual for a single flower to be six inches in diameter. Blooms last up to two weeks and a *Cattleya* usually puts out from one to three flowers at a time.

Cattleyas need repotting every two to three years, when their potting mix has decomposed enough to no longer provide adequate aeration for the plant's roots. Wait until after your *Cattleya* has flowered to repot the plant. Many *Cattleyas* flower in spring, so repot these in early summer, before new roots start to form on the new pseudobulbs. A good general rule is to repot your orchid a week or two after it has stopped blooming.

At some point your *Cattleya* will need a larger pot. If you don't have room for a bigger plant on your windowsill, try dividing your orchid. Follow the directions provided in "*Cattleya* Makeover" (Chapter Seven), and after step number five, cut the horizontal stem from which the pseudobulbs grow. Make sure that each **division** has at least three vertical growths, so each small plant will be able to support itself. Then continue with step number six of the makeover process.

Many other types of orchid are hybridized with *Cattleya* species. These hybrids are frequently called *Cattleyas*, although their full names are long agglomerations of their different parents' names. They all have similar cultural requirements, and are members of . . . the *Cattleya* Alliance.

LIGHT REQUIREMENTS

LOW LIGHT = indirect light, as in an unobstructed northern window, or an eastern window surrounded by buildings or trees
MEDIUM LIGHT = bright, indirect light as in an unobstructed eastern or western window with a sheer curtain
HIGH LIGHT = bright, direct light as in a western or southern window

Orchids for Wimps	Low	Medium	High
Phalaenopsis	X	X	
Paphiopedilum	X	X	
Brassavola nodosa		X	X
Dendrobium		X	X
Oncidium		X	X
Cattleya		X	X
Cattleya Alliance		X	X
Dendrochilum magnum		X	X
Phragmipedium		X	
Ludisia & other jewel orchids	X	X	
Miltonia		X	
Encyclia cochleata		X	X
Brassia		X	X
Doritis pulcherrima		X	
Cochleanthes amazonica	X	X	
Gongora quinquenervis		X	

The *Cattleya* Alliance

It sounds like a futuristic political coalition: "We have made first contact with a new civilization. They call themselves . . . The *Cattleya* Alliance." In fact, the *Cattleya* (Cat-láy-ah) Alliance includes many species and hybrid orchids, all of which have **cultural** requirements similar to those of the *Cattleya* species. The group also includes **intergeneric** hybrids, which are frequently called "*Cattleyas*" because their full names are long and complicated.

For homegrowers, orchids in this group are a wonderful choice. Many are smaller than members of the *Cattleya* genus and fit perfectly on a sunny windowsill. Their exquisite jewel tones are vibrant and saturated, and range from vermilion to lavender. Many have multiple blooms that last four weeks, and I must confess, some of my very favorite orchids are members of the alliance.

(ABOVE): *Brassolaeliocattleya* Waiana King (TOP RIGHT): *Potinara* Flash Dance (BOTTOM RIGHT): *Sophrolaeliocattleya* Jungle Jewel

Abbreviation	Full name	Parentage
Bc.	*Brassocattleya*	*Brassavola* x *Cattleya*
Bl.	*Brassolaelia*	*Brassavola* x *Laelia*
Blc.	*Brassolaeliocattleya*	*Brassavola* x *Laelia* x *Cattleya*
Lc.	*Laeliocattleya*	*Laelia* x *Cattleya*
Low.	*Lowara*	*Brassavola* x *Sophronitis* x *Laelia*
Pot.	*Potinara*	*Brassavola* x *Cattleya* x *Laelia* x *Sophronitis*
Sl.	*Sophrolaelia*	*Sophronitis* x *Laelia*
Slc.	*Sophrolaeliocattleya*	*Sophronitis* x *Laelia* x *Cattleya*

(LEFT): *Sophrolaeliocattleya* Crystelle Smith 'Rosalie' (BOTTOM): *Brassocattleya* g. Star Reiby cv. Xanadu

(TOP): *Laeliocattleya* **Jungle Elf** (BOTTOM): *Brassolaelia* **Angel Lace 'Breckenridge'**

Various *Cattleya* Alliance genera are used in hybridization for their distinctive characteristics. *Cattleyas* contribute a large flower size, *Laelia* orchids are used for their multiple bloom habit, *Sophronitis* flowers are valued for their shape and bright colors, and *Brassavola* is used for its large, showy lip. In general, flowers of these "*Cattleyas*" last for four to six weeks, and many make excellent cut flowers. Some are also wonderfully fragrant, like *Bc.* Angel Lace 'Breckenridge' with its lovely grape smell, *Lc.* Jungle Elk with its complex fruity aroma, and *Bl.* 'Morning Glory,' which smells like fresh candy.

The tags on these intergeneric hybrids often give only the abbreviation of the genus name, since the full names would be difficult to fit on a small piece of plastic. The table on page 62 explains which **genera** are crossed to give you the different hybrid members of the *Cattleya* Alliance. If you're not particularly interested in the pedigree of your orchid, you can ignore the nomenclature and note that, generally, all members of the *Cattleya* Alliance can be grown in *Cattleya*-friendly conditions: high light, nighttime temperatures in the 55° to 60°F range, and a quick-draining potting medium that dries out between waterings.

Dendrochilum magnum

Dendrochilum magnum (den-dro-kígh-lumm mág-num) is known as the golden chain orchid, and one look tells you why. The long bloom spikes are dramatic, with their dangling double rows of tiny flowers. Spikes can have up to a hundred individual blooms, each about one-quarter inch across, and the "chains" can be twelve inches long. *Dendrochilums* are also wonderfully fragrant and can fill a room with their citrus perfume.

Because of their remarkable pendant bloom habit, *Dendrochilums* look especially wonderful hanging or displayed on a tall plant stand, where their chains can really be appreciated. These orchids bloom once a year, usually in fall, and each chain lasts for two to three weeks.

Golden chain orchids have pseudobulbs, which indicate that they are drought-tolerant. This water storage tissue allows them to survive the dry season in their native habitat. Each pseudobulb is topped by a single leaf and can produce a bloom spike, so it's not unusual for a single plant to produce many chains.

Older plants make a particularly dramatic display with their many spikes, so rather than divide these plants, keep them large and showy. They'll need repotting about every two years and no additional grooming is necessary other than cutting off the flower spikes once they have finished blooming.

These orchids have light requirements similar to *Cattleyas*, in other words, they like lots of sun. They'll bloom best in a southern or western window but can also flower in bright eastern light. Normal household temperatures are fine for the golden chain orchid, but don't let it get colder than 55°F. These plants are native to Southeast Asia where it's hot and humid.

Dendrochilums are epiphytes and can be mounted on bark slabs or potted in a quick-draining bark mix. Like *Cattleyas*, which also have pseudobulbs, golden chain orchids like to dry out between waterings. In summer you'll need to water two or three times a week, depending on temperatures and humidity. (Higher heat or lower humidity means they need more frequent watering.) In winter, watering once a week should be adequate. Be sure not to let your *Dendrochilum* stay constantly damp, or root rot may set in.

Even when a *Dendrochilum* is not in flower, it's a nice-looking tropical houseplant. But when the golden chain orchid is in bloom it is spectacular and fragrant, a worthy centerpiece in anyone's orchid collection.

Dendrochilum magnum

Phragmipedium

It's only a matter of time until *Phragmipedium* (frag-mih-pée-dee-um) orchids take the world by storm. These beauties are easy to care for, have dramatic good looks, and their flowers last for weeks. They come in a wide variety of colors, from electrifying vermilion to shell pink to canary yellow. Many *Phragmipediums* bloom in winter, brightening up anybody's dark days. These orchids are irresistible; try one and you'll be hooked.

Phragmipediums, also known as Phrags, are closely related to *Paphiopedilum* orchids. Both have a rounded pouch and the same basic shape. While *Paphiopedilum* leaves can be either green or mottled, *Phragmipedium* leaves are always green and more upright than *Paphiopedilum* foliage. Phrags also have longer bloom spikes, up to thirty inches tall, and their flowers open in succession, from the bottom up. Each flower lasts for one to two weeks, so a single bloom spike can provide color for months. It's not unusual to have several flowers on a single spike in bloom simultaneously.

Phragmipediums are terrestrial orchids. In nature they benefit from almost constant moisture and a growing medium rich in humus. This gives us two important clues regarding *Phragmipedium* culture. First, high levels of humus indicate that *Phragmipediums* are heavier feeders

Phragmipedium richterii

WATER REQUIREMENTS

The frequency with which you should water your orchid depends on so many things: time of year, type of pot, room temperature, and ambient humidity, to name a few. It's important to develop a feel for when your orchid needs water, rather than stick to a strict schedule. In general, drought tolerant orchids will need watering every 7-10 days and less drought tolerant orchids will require water every 3-5 days. Use these suggestions as a starting point and adjust as necessary.

Orchids for Wimps	Drought Tolerant	In Between	Not Drought Tolerant
Phalaenopsis		X	
Paphiopedilum			X
Brassavola nodosa	X		
Dendrobium		X	
Oncidium		X	
Cattleya	X		
Cattleya Alliance	X		
Dendrochilum magnum		X	
Phragmipedium			X
Ludisia & other jewel orchids		X	
Miltonia		X	
Encyclia cochleata		X	
Brassia		X	
Doritis pulcherrima		X	
Cochleanthes amazonica		X	
Gongora quinquenervis		X	

than many other orchids. They can be fed every week during the growing season. Second, Phrags should be kept damp at all times; their roots should never be allowed to dry out.

Water your *Phragmipedium* orchid two to three times a week in warm weather, and once a week in the cool season. After watering, they should be allowed to sit in a saucer of water. The water will gradually be absorbed by the potting medium, and the saucer should be refilled if all the water evaporates between waterings.

Fertilizers can accumulate in both the potting medium and the saucer of water, so be sure to completely **flush** the root system of your Phrag each time you water it. This is simple: Water the orchid until water pours out into the saucer, empty the run-off, then fill the saucer with fresh water. If the roots are not flushed and fertilizers build up in the potting medium, the orchid's roots can be burned and will gradually die back. Dead leaf tips are an indication of this problem.

Because Phrags like to remain constantly moist, it's best to pot them in plastic, which slows the evaporation of water from the potting mix. If you don't like the way plastic looks, you can slip the plastic pot inside a **cachepot** that better suits your decor. Since so many orchids are watered to death, it's nice to know that there's an orchid you can't overwater. You may have to water a *Phragmipedium* slightly more frequently than you'll water a *Cattleya*, but you won't have to worry about giving it too much.

Phragmipedium orchids flower best in medium light, so an eastern or western window is recommended. Their leaves will be dark green if they don't get enough light and yellow if they get too much. If light levels are not high enough, your plant may not flower, although its foliage can still look healthy.

The more frequent watering schedule required by

(LEFT): *Phragmipedium besseae* (TOP RIGHT): *Phragmipedium schlimii* (BOTTOM RIGHT): *Phragmipedium* Cardinale

Phragmipediums leads to a faster decomposition of its potting mix. As a result, Phrags need repotting more frequently than many other orchids: they will benefit from repotting every year after flowering. If Phrags are left in a mix that has decomposed too heavily, their roots will deteriorate and be unable to provide nutrition for the orchid.

As long as you remember to water them more frequently, you can grow *Phragmipediums* alongside more drought-tolerant orchids with similar light requirements (like *Oncidiums, Dendrobiums, Cattleyas*, etc.). The ease of care and the rewarding blooms of the *Phragmipedium* are bound to make them one of the most popular tropical orchids.

Ludisia Discolor and Other Jewel-Type Orchids

Jewel orchids don't look like typical orchids. Pass one on the street, and you'd think it belonged to a completely different family. But these little gems are extremely easy to grow and bloom, and their foliage is among the most beautiful in the orchid family.

Ludisia discolor (lew-dée-zia dis-co-lóre) is commonly called the jewel orchid, and unlike most orchids, it's prized for its outstanding foliage rather than for its flowers. Its leaves are velvety-black with red markings, and its growth habit is wide and spreading. When potted, the stems and leaves will cascade over the edge of the pot as they grow, making a dramatic display. *Ludisia* blooms in fall and winter, bearing spikes of numerous small white and yellow flowers which contrast nicely with the plant's dark foliage. Each stem usually produces a bloom spike, so a large plant in flower can look quite dramatic.

Ludisia is a terrestrial orchid; in nature its jointed stems creep along the forest floor, rooting in decaying leaves and humus. Because of its terrestrial origins, you might expect *Ludisia* to need more frequent watering than many of its epiphytic relatives. On the contrary, it is fairly drought-tolerant; its fleshy stems retain water for times of drought. In spring and summer, water your *Ludisia* once every five to seven days. In winter, it can go ten days without watering.

Ludisia discolor 'Negra'

Ludisia does not require a bark-based mix, as so many other orchids do, and can be grown in regular houseplant potting mix. It is also very easy to propagate. If you break off a piece of the jewel orchid, simply stick the stem in a glass of water. Within a few weeks you'll see roots growing from the stem and you can gently plant the piece back in its original pot, or plant it by itself and give it to a friend.

There is one thing to be extremely careful of with the jewel orchid: Don't let its leaves get wet. Water on the leaves can cause white spots or streaks, marring the beauty of Ludisia's foliage. This means no misting, so keep Ludisia on a drywell to achieve the higher humidity that almost all orchids require.

Recently, another jewel-type orchid, Stennorrhynchos speciosa (sten-oh-ríne-kos spee-see-óh-sa), has become very popular. Its leaves grow in a rosette and are beautifully spotted with white dots. Bloom spikes grow about eighteen inches tall and produce clusters of small, brilliant red flowers that last four to six weeks. This orchid blooms around Christmas time, and its holiday colors make it a wonderful alternative to the ubiquitous Poinsettia.

Keep your jewel orchids out of direct sunlight. Ludisia leaves fade if given too much light. They will grow and flower well in eastern or bright northern exposures, but you may need to protect them from the sun's rays in an eastern window. Stennorrhynchos can take slightly more light; an eastern or western window would be best.

(LEFT): *Ludisia discolor* (TOP AND BOTTOM RIGHT): *Stennorrhynchos speciosa*

Miltonia

Miltonia (mill-tóe-nee-ya) orchids are frequently called pansy orchids because their charming flowers are flat and open, with a distinctive central "mask" of a contrasting color. *Miltonias* can flower several times during the year, and their blooms last three to four weeks. However, flowers wilt very quickly after being cut, so don't plan on using *Miltonias* in a bouquet.

Pansy orchids do well in regular household temperatures and are easy to grow if a few basic requirements are met. Unlike many other orchids, *Miltonias* do not grow most actively in warm weather, and, in fact, grow best if kept below 80°F. In fall, they grow more rapidly, and temperatures between 70° and 80°F should be maintained. This may be your normal household temperature already. After flowering is complete, try to give your pansy orchid nighttime temperatures of 55° to 60°F. This should be attainable in a large window.

In nature, *Miltonias* are epiphytes and grow in dappled sunlight. In your home, protect them from direct sun by placing them in an eastern window, or behind a sheer curtain in western or southern light. Too much light will actually inhibit their ability to flower.

Pansy orchids have small pseudobulbs, but, unlike many orchids with pseudobulbs, they should not be allowed to dry out between waterings. Their foliage is thin and sensitive. If new leaves emerge looking pleated like an accordion, this is a sign of too little water. Increase your watering frequency, and subsequent leaves should grow

(TOP): *Miltonia* **Red Woodham cv. Wendy** (BOTTOM): *Miltonia* g. **Saopaulo**

flat, although the earlier, wrinkled leaves will not flatten out. In warm weather, you'll probably need to water your *Miltonia* two or three times a week. In cooler weather, once every five to seven days should be sufficient. Grow the pansy orchid in a quick-draining bark mix and place it on a drywell for that all-important high humidity.

Another genus of orchids, *Miltoniopsis*, was grouped with the genus *Miltonias* for years but is now recognized as a separate group of orchids with somewhat different growing requirements. *Miltoniopsis* require cooler growing temperatures, less light, and higher humidity than *Miltonias*, and may be somewhat more difficult for the home grower to bloom. (If you decide to try growing *Miltoniopsis*, you'll be rewarded with sweet fragrance as well as beautiful bloom.) Both groups are abbreviated "Milt.," so ask the seller exactly which kind of orchid it is. Many hybrids of *Miltonia* and *Miltoniopsis* do well in a home environment.

Miltonia orchids are easily hybridized and many extraordinary intergeneric hybrids have *Miltonias* as a parent.

- *Miltonidiums* are a cross between *Miltonia* and *Oncidium* orchids, and for me, it was love at first sight. These are compact plants, perfectly suited to windowsill culture, and their numerous small flowers grow on multibranched sprays. The bloom spikes are often larger than the foliage, and the bright colors of

(TOP LEFT): *Miltoniopsis* **Firewater (TOP RIGHT):** *Miltonidium* **Pupukea Sunset (BOTTOM RIGHT):** *Colmanara* **Wildcat 'Bob'**

their blooms are irresistible. Plants bloom once or twice a year and their flowers last three to four weeks.

- *Colmanara* hybrids are a combination of *Miltonia*, *Odontoglossum*, and *Oncidium* orchids. The flower shape looks like that of the *Miltonia*, while the growth habit of the plant more closely resembles that of its other forebears. Flowers open on tall spikes, last four to eight weeks, and are dramatically speckled gold and mahogany.

Encyclia cochleata

Encyclia cochleata (en-síck-lee-yah coke-lee-áh-tah) is commonly known as the octopus orchid and one look will tell you why. Yellow-green tepals hang down like graceful tentacles from a shell-shaped lip that sits on top like a mantilla and can be either dark purple or pale yellow-green. It's got several other common names, like the clamshell orchid and the cockleshell orchid, but I think "octopus" is the most descriptive. *Encyclia cochleata* has a unique flower; nothing else even vaguely resembles it. It's very easy to grow and has an exceptionally long blooming season.

This is a plant that truly gets better with age. A young *Encyclia cochleata* may produce one or two flowers on a bloom stalk. The older the plant, the taller the bloom spike, and the more flowers it will produce. The flowers don't all open at once, but rather in succession, and spikes can have up to a hundred flowers that can bloom for a full year!

The octopus orchid is a miniature *Encyclia* and fits well on a small windowsill. Like the *Cattleya*, *Encyclia cochleata* grows best in high light; a western or southern window will be best for bloom. In fact, the octopus orchid shares many cultural requirements with *Cattleyas*. It is an epiphyte and grows best in a quick-draining bark mix that provides good root aeration. *Encyclia cochleata* has prominent pseudobulbs, and is somewhat drought-tolerant. It should be allowed to dry out between waterings and likes high humidity. During warm weather, this orchid should be watered twice a week. In winter, once a week may be adequate. If the pseudobulbs look wrinkled or shriveled, increase the frequency of your watering by one day every two weeks until the bulbs again look plump.

Encyclia cochleata is a highly adaptable orchid that does not require special thermostat manipulation, one more reason it makes such an easy house guest. It can tolerate nighttime temperatures of 50°F and daytime highs of up to 95°F. In other words, a large, bright window should be perfect.

Until fairly recently, *Encyclia cochleata* was known as *Epidendrum cochleatum*, so don't be confused if you see this little beauty labeled with its old name. There's no other orchid like it; if you see an octopus shaped flower, grab it and go.

Encyclia cochleata

Brassia don't come in a wide range of colors but their markings are strikingly beautiful. They are gold or green with speckles and bands of purple or maroon. Their spidery legs can be anywhere from one to twelve inches long, depending on the species.

Most *Brassia* orchids are epiphytes and have large pseudobulbs, making them relatively drought-tolerant orchids. They grow best with high humidity, so be sure to place them on drywells, but don't mist the *pseudobulbs*, which can rot. *Brassias* like lots of water during spring and summer: twice or three times a week depending on how hot and dry your home is. When the growing season ends, *Brassias* will rest for about two months as they get ready to flower. During this time, watering once a week is sufficient.

Spider orchids do well on a bright windowsill, but should not be given too much direct sun. Eastern or western light is preferable, but if you must give it southern light, protect your *Brassia* from direct rays by hanging a sheer curtain. Nighttime temperatures of 55° to 60°F and daytime temperatures of around 75°F will produce the most profuse flowering.

Brassias roots have a tendency to grow across the top of the potting mix, which is normal. Don't interpret this as a signal that repotting is necessary. *Brassias* prefer not to have their roots disturbed, so don't repot more than once every three years. Then, do so as soon as the plant has finished blooming. These epiphytes should be potted in a quick-draining mix, and can be fed every two weeks during the growing season with a balanced fertilizer.

(LEFT): **Brassia Rex 'Sakata'** (RIGHT): **The roots of Brassia Rex 'Sakata' grow across the top of the potting mix.**

Brassia

Brassia (bráss-ee-ah) orchids are dramatically spiky, and their long sprays of large, exotic flowers immediately command your attention. Their common name is spider orchid, which comes from the long, slender sepals and petals radiating out from every flower. Bloom spikes can get very large, extending three or four feet beyond the plant itself. Some *Brassia* orchids bloom twice a year, and their flowers last from four to eight weeks. This plant is a definite eye-catcher, and in case that isn't enough, many are wonderfully fragrant.

(TOP LEFT, TOP RIGHT, BOTTOM LEFT): *Odontobrassia* **Pisgah Recluse** (BOTTOM RIGHT): *Miltassia* **Charles Fitch**

Brassia orchids are easily hybridized with several other **genera** of orchids. The resulting hybrids require basically the same care as the *Brassia* orchids. *Miltassia* orchids are a hybrid of *Miltonias* and *Brassias* and combine the dramatic shape of the *Brassia* with the wonderful colors of the *Miltonias*. *Odontobrassia* orchids are a cross between *Brassia* and *Odontoglossum* orchids, and *Brassidium* orchids are the result of a *Brassia-Oncidium* pairing. All of these hybrids produce long-lasting, dramatic bloom.

Doritis are useful in hybridization and are most frequently bred with *Phalaenopsis* orchids, resulting in hybrids that are called *Doritaenopsis*. *Doritaenopsis* look very similar to Phals but inherit several interesting characteristics from *Doritis pulcherrima*, including their summer bloom habit. If you see what looks like a summer-blooming Phal, it's probably a *Doritaenopsis*. Also, *Doritaenopsis* have more upright blooms than *Phalaenopsis*, showing the influence of *Doritis's* very vertical flower stalk.

Doritis can take slightly more light than *Phalaenopsis*, so an eastern or western window is best. In a southern exposure the orchid benefits from some protection, so hang a sheer curtain between the plant and the glass. This orchid won't bloom in a northern window.

The foliage of *Doritis pulcherrima* is smaller than *Phalaenopsis* foliage, but similar in shape, color, and thickness. It does not have pseudobulbs for water storage, but its thicker-than-average leaves are capable of retaining moisture. *Doritis* should be potted in a medium bark mixture that provides both adequate moisture and root aeration.

Doritis pulcherrima should be watered every five to seven days in summer and every seven to ten days in winter. It benefits from the extra humidity provided by a drywell, and during the bud stage high humidity will improve flower production. Normal household temperatures are fine for this orchid; just make sure night temperatures don't drop below 60°F when the buds are forming.

Doritis pulcherrima

Doritis pulcherrima (dor-íte-is pull-kuh-ríme-ah) is a dainty little thing with a surprisingly tough constitution. Its miniature stature makes it well suited to windowsill growing, and it rivals the *Phalaenopsis* orchids for ease of care. Although there is only one species of *Doritis*, there are several varieties, and flower colors can range from cerise to lavender to delicate shell pink with pale orange-yellow accents. *Doritis* bloom on slender spikes about eighteen inches tall, and may flower several times a year. Individual blooms open a few at a time and last for several weeks; the entire spike can last several months as flowers pass in and out of bloom.

Doritis usually bloom in summer, so remember this when you're adding to your orchid collection. It's not always easy to find a summer-blooming orchid and it's nice to have something in bloom all year round. *Doritis pulcherrima* will add color to your windowsill for several months in warm weather.

(LEFT): **Doritis pulcherrima "chumpornensis" 'Lakeview'** (RIGHT): **Doritaenopsis Brother Tom Walsh**

Cochleanthes amazonica

OK, I admit the name is a mouthful, but this is a gorgeous orchid. It blooms easily and frequently in the home, and is an excellent choice for the beginner. I bought my first *Cochleanthes amazonica* (Coke-lee-án-thees ah-ma-zón-ih-ka) in mid-October in full bloom, and in mid-January it was already blooming again. The flowers are huge compared to the overall size of the plant: a five-inch tall orchid bears three-inch flowers. They are pristine white, marked at the center with thin stripes of deep purple, and have a wonderful, spicy scent.

Cochleanthes amazonica bears its flowers on short bloom stalks that are wonderfully set off against rich green foliage. This orchid is free-flowering for a good part of the year, and its blooms last for three to four weeks. It usually starts to bloom in fall, and it flowers off and on until late spring. As a rule, *Cochleanthes amazonica* doesn't bloom in summer, but will put out new foliage at this time.

Like *Phalaenopsis*, *Cochleanthes amazonica* is a low-to-medium light orchid and grows best in an eastern window. In nature, it is a low-growing epiphyte and will be found low in the canopy where light is heavily dappled. Normal household temperatures are just fine for this plant; try not to let nighttime temperatures drop below 60°F.

You'll notice that *Cochleanthes amazonica* does not have pseudobulbs, nor are its leaves thick and waxy, like those of the genus *Phalaenopsis*. The lack of pseudobulbs combined with its thin foliage tell you that this orchid cannot store much water as a reserve. Therefore, they should never be allowed to dry out completely. (Don't forget, if you notice new leaves emerging with an accordionlike fold, you should water your orchid more frequently.) The folded leaves will not straighten out, but new leaves will come in straight once the watering schedule has been correctly adjusted. In summer, this orchid will probably need watering two or three times a week. In winter, once a week should be sufficient.

Cochleanthes amazonica can be grown in either a pot or orchid box. A quick-draining bark mix, thoroughly and frequently watered, will be best for this orchid, since despite its need for constant moisture, you should not let its roots stay wet. Don't allow standing water to accumulate in the leaf axils, or rot may become a problem.

This miniature orchid is perfectly suited to windowsill culture, and the ease with which it blooms makes it an excellent "confidence-builder" for the beginner. It's a triple threat: beautiful color, enticing scent, and frequent bloom. What's not to like?

Cochleanthes amazonica

Gongora quinquenervis

The flowers of this orchid remind me of a jeweled earring hanging gracefully in midair. Blooms are combinations of different reds and yellows, and these rich colors are complemented by a pleasant, spicy scent. It's not unusual for this orchid to bloom twice a year. The bloom stalks grow from the base of the orchid's pseudobulbs and curve downward, holding the flowers below the foliage, alongside the pot itself. This exotic orchid is not difficult to grow, and its unique appearance makes it an excellent addition to any orchid collection.

Gongora quinquenervis (gone-gó-rah kwin-kwuh-nérv-us) is a charming small orchid, perfectly suited to windowsill culture. The older it gets, the more flower stalks it will put out, and a five-inch pot may display six to eight bloom spikes at a time. The length of a single stalk is frequently greater than the height of the foliage.

All *Gongora* species are epiphytes, and in a home environment they grow best potted in a quick-draining bark mix. In nature they thrive in semi-shade, and in your home they will flourish in medium light, similar to that appropriate for the *Phalaenopsis*. An eastern window would be best. Normal household temperatures are fine for *Gongora quinquenervis*. Its only special requirement is the high humidity you can easily provide by growing this orchid on a drywell.

When *Gongora quinquenervis* starts to bloom, you may want to show off its pendant flowers by hanging the plant where its unusual growth habit can be best appreciated. It's perfectly all right to move the plant from its drywell for the duration of its bloom (approximately two weeks). Just be sure to replace it on the drywell when the flowers have died, so it can resume growing in a more humid atmosphere.

Gongora quinquenervis

Gongora quinquenervis has ridged pseudobulbs and thin leaves with prominent veins. While pseudobulbs usually indicate the ability to store water for times of drought, *Gongora* grows best if never allowed to completely dry out between waterings. This means watering two or three times a week in the heat of summer, and once or twice a week during the cooler times of year, depending on the temperature in your home.

Gongora should be fed regularly with a balanced fertilizer. Start feeding in spring, every other week, with a solution half as strong as recommended on the fertilizer package. When the growing season ends (usually in mid-autumn, depending on your location), stop fertilizing for the remainder of the year.

You might try growing this orchid on a small glass shelf in a sunny kitchen window at or above eye level. This way, the blooms can hang down in plain view, and fill the air with their spicy scent.

Gongora quinquenervis

BLOOM FREQUENCY AND DURATION

Some orchids can bloom continuously for months at a time. The following table will help you choose orchids so you can always have something in bloom.

Orchids for Wimps	Bloom Season	Bloom Duration
Phalaenopsis	Fall – Spring	1–6 months
Paphiopedilum	Fall – Spring	2–3 months
Brassavola nodosa	Fall – Spring	4–6 weeks
Dendrobium	Fall – Winter	1–2 months
Oncidium	year round (depending on species)	1–2 months
Cattleya	Spring – Fall	2 weeks
Cattleya Alliance	year round (depending on species)	2–4 weeks
Dendrochilum magnum	Fall	2–3 weeks
Phragmipedium	Winter – Spring	1–2 months
Ludisia & other jewel orchids	Fall – Winter	2–4 weeks
Miltonia	Summer – Fall	4–6 weeks
Encyclia cochleata	Spring – Fall	1 month
Brassia	Spring – Summer	1 month
Doritis pulcherrima	Summer	2–4 weeks
Cochleanthes amazonica	Fall – Winter	1 month
Gongora quinquenervis	Winter & Summer (twice a year)	2 weeks

Of course, some orchids are difficult to grow and need careful temperature manipulation or daily misting and watering. But since there are so many lower-maintenance orchids to choose from, it's easy to avoid the prima donnas and concentrate on more accommodating plants.

Has your head been turned by an enticing seductress? Take a step back and ask yourself what it is that you find so appealing. Is it the color, the shape, the scent? There's almost always an easygoing orchid that shares some of the most endearing characteristics of the high-maintenance diva. Why not choose a plant that builds your orchid-growing confidence, rather than one that severely challenges your newfound ability to grow?

Chapter 5

Don't
Try These
at Home

Masdevallia **Dean Haas**

Masdevallia

There's no doubt about it, this is a spectacular orchid. The colors are rich and saturated, and its sepals are greatly elongated, getting slimmer as they lengthen until they fade away into nothing. Unfortunately, *Masdevallias* are cool-growing orchids and require nighttime temperatures of about 45°F, which is colder than most of us can provide. Also, temperatures above 80°F can prevent this orchid from blooming. Humidity should be maintained at over 60%, and these plants require good air movement around their roots and foliage, which usually must be provided by small fans. Sounds complicated? Why not try growing a ***Psychopsis*** instead?

Psychopsis

These orchids grow well in normal household temperatures and will flower in any exposure except northern. They are frequently called butterfly orchids due to their unusual shape and elongated petals and sepals. Flowers open one at a time on long stalks, and a single plant can be in bloom for several months. Even after the flowers have died, leave the stalk in place, because it may rebloom. *Psychopsis* was once classified as an *Oncidium*, and its cultural requirements are similar to those of that genus: good light, quick-draining potting mix, and the chance to dry out between waterings.

(LEFT): ***Psychopsis kalihi* (yellow)** and ***Psychopsis papilo* 'Breckenridge' (orange)**

80

(LEFT): *Stanhopea species*

Stanhopea

These orchids have a very unusual growth habit: their bloom spikes grow down from the base of the pseudo-bulbs and are best displayed when grown in wire baskets so the flower stalk can actually poke out the bottom of the basket. Blooms are large and unusually shaped, and most have strong scents, which range from spicy to foul. Flowers last only a day, and these orchids should never be allowed to dry out. They also grow best if given a month-long rest period (reduced water and slightly cooler temperatures) after blooming. If keeping a wire basket constantly moist in your home sounds like too much trouble, consider growing a **Gongora**.

Gongora

The flowers of this orchid are similar in shape to those of *Stanhopea*. However, they last longer, are not foul-smelling, and they cascade over the side of your pot rather than burrowing through the potting medium. No rest period is required after blooming and they prosper in less light than the *Stanhopea*. Also, *Gongora* is a considerably smaller plant and easily fits on a narrow windowsill or shelf, while *Stanhopea* can get quite large and needs to be hung.

(ABOVE AND RIGHT): *Gongora quinquenervis*

(ABOVE AND TOP LEFT): *Phalandopsis* **Arizona Star (***Vanda* **alliance) (TOP RIGHT):** *Vanda* **roots in basket without potting mix**

Vanda/Phalandopsis

Admit it, you've fallen in love with a *Vanda* (or one of its close relatives). You were walking down the street, you passed the florist's, looked in the window, and now it's all you can think about. Who can blame you? These are spectacular orchids with vivid colors and tightly overlapping leaves that form a wonderful pattern even when the orchid isn't in bloom. If you live in Florida or Hawaii, and have a large arbor out back where you can hang this plant, then by all means, go for it. However, if you live someplace more temperate, wait a minute. These are tall plants, easily reaching four feet. Will this fit on your windowsill? *Vandas* need almost full sun. This means not behind glass, which reduces the intensity of the rays that reach the plant. They also require very high humidity, and should be grown on bark or in orchid boxes without potting mix. This all adds up to daily care. Are you really ready for this kind of high-maintenance relationship, or would you be better off with an *Ascocentrum*?

Ascocentrum Sagarik Gold

This beauty is also a member of the *Vanda* Alliance (what, you thought there was only one Alliance in all of orchid-dom?) and shares many characteristics with her taller, thinner sister. First of all, its outstanding flower color rivals the best of the orange *Vandas*. Second, its foliage grows in the same overlapping pattern as the *Vandas*. And while *Ascocentrum* also prefers high humidity, it has a more compact growth habit and does well potted in a bark-based mix. *Ascocentrum Sagarik Gold* requires temperatures and light levels similar to those appropriate for *Cattleyas*.

(TOP AND BOTTOM): *Ascocentrum* **Sagarik Gold**

Cymbidium hybrids

Cymbidiums are large plants with grasslike foliage and multiple spikes of numerous, long-lasting, big, beautiful, flowers. Sounds great, right? Unfortunately, *Cymbidiums* like their temperatures a little cooler than most human beings do. Nighttime temperatures of 45°F are recommended for optimum bloom, and daytime temperatures over 75°F can inhibit blooming altogether. Some new, miniature hybrids are more tolerant of temperatures up to 80°F, but in general, *Cymbidiums* require cool growing conditions. Also, these orchids are not easy to place, due to their size. They are usually sold in ten- or twelve-inch pots and are about three feet tall. *Cymbidium* flowers are roundish, last for a few weeks, and come in a range of colors including pinks, yellows, and creams, similar to those of the much easier to grow **Phalaenopsis**.

Cymbidium **hybrids**

Phalaenopsis

Phalaenopsis hybrids are low-maintenance orchids whose flowers last for months. They thrive in normal household temperatures and survive on once-a-week watering. While they appreciate the elevated humidity provided by a drywell, they are more tolerant of average humidity than most other orchids. Their flowers are available in numerous colors and sizes, some with captivating patterns of stripes and dots. *Phalaenopsis* foliage does not resemble the upright grassy leaves of the *Cymbidium*, but it is beautiful, and dramatically sculptural. There are so many wonderful varieties of *Phalaenopsis*, you could compose an entire orchid collection out of just this one genus.

(TOP): *Phalaenopsis* hybrid (LEFT): *Phalaenopsis* Kathleen Ai x Phalaenopsis gigantea (BELOW): *Phalaenopsis* Mini Mark x *Phalaenopsis* Philippience

If you've been paying attention, you know by now that light and humidity are two of the most important concepts to master if you want to grow orchids successfully. (If you haven't been paying attention, go back to the beginning and start over!) Unfortunately, they're also two things that may seem difficult to control in a home environment. What if your apartment or house is dark? How can you change the amount of sun that comes in through the windows? You can't. And what about humidity? Summer isn't so tough, but when the heat goes on in winter, forget it. The air can be so dry, it hurts when you breathe.

Actually, there are several things you can do to improve the light and humidity in small, manageable parts of your home, rather than tackling the entire establishment at once. Light and humidity can both be improved without enormous expense, and the results are priceless.

Chapter 6

Improving

Growing

Conditions

A mercury vapor 150-watt light bulb gives off a high intensity light appropriate for this *Epicattleya* Rene Marques 'Flamethrower.'

Let there be light.

While some orchids grow and flower in low to medium light, many more require at least a few hours of bright light every day in order to bloom. But your ability to grow and flower orchids doesn't have to be limited by your access to natural light. Even if your apartment only has a northern exposure, or if your growing space is across the room from the nearest window, all is not lost.

There have been great improvements in artificial light in the past five to ten years, so the absence of sunlight should not limit your orchid growing. Many of the orchids described in this book have compact growth habits and fit easily under lights. Add an inexpensive timer to any light fixture and you won't have to worry

about remembering to turn your light garden off and on. It's an especially good idea to keep your orchids on drywells if you're growing them under lights. The energy emitted by the light bulbs raises temperatures and lowers humidity around the plants.

There are several different kinds of bulbs appropriate for growing orchids. Before you decide which is best for you, consider the following things:

Color: While the sun emits light in all colors of the visible spectrum, light in the blue and red ranges is most important for plant growth. Flowering plants require large amounts of orange/red light in order to bloom, and blue light promotes lush, compact growth of foliage plants.

Intensity: Light intensity is the strength of the light emitted by a light source. Accordingly, plants that share the light of a single fixture should have similar light requirements. Orchids can be raised closer to the bulb for increased light intensity by placing them on top of overturned pots, and orchids with lower light requirements can be placed at the edges of the growing area, where less intense light is cast.

Duration: This refers to the number of hours of light a plant gets per day. The light from grow-bulbs is less intense than sunlight, so we compensate by giving orchids growing under bulbs more hours of light than they would receive in nature. Increased quantity compensates for reduced intensity. Because plants also require a rest period, don't leave the lights on all day long. Fourteen to sixteen hours of light per day should be about right.

If you're just starting out, fluorescent tubes are an excellent choice. They are inexpensive and can be used in tabletop fixtures or ceiling lamps. You can use a combination of warm and cool tubes, or opt for the slightly more expensive, full-spectrum fluorescent tubes, which emit a more natural-looking light.

Full-spectrum bulbs are available in 24" and 48" lengths, which are standard sizes for grow-light fixtures. They emit light with a quality equivalent to noon sunlight.

Fluorescent lights are best used with curved reflectors that direct maximum light toward the plants. Inexpensive shop-light fixtures with flat reflectors also reflect considerable light onto orchids below. All fluorescent bulbs give off less light from the ends of the tubes than from the center. Plants requiring lower light should be placed

(TOP LEFT AND RIGHT): **Fluorescent lights are inexpensive and a good way to start growing with artificial lights.** (BOTTOM LEFT): **Incandescent grow-bulbs give a less intense light appropriate for** *Phalaenopsis* **orchids.**

under the three inches of tube at either end of the fixture. Additionally, fluorescent tubes in use for approximately sixteen hours per day should be replaced every eighteen months.

High Intensity Discharge (HID) lamps are the brightest lights available and include Metal Halide (MH) and High Pressure Sodium (HPS) bulbs. If you discover you enjoy growing under artificial lights, you may want to invest in an HID system. These lights run on normal household voltages, but require special fixtures and are more complicated to install than fluorescent lights. However, high-light orchids will thrive under the intense light of HID lamps.

Metal halide bulbs give off light that is strongest at the blue end of the spectrum and looks most like natural sunlight. This light produces compact, leafy growth and is preferable when your light garden is an integral part of your home, since the light does not distort the colors of the plants (and people) it illuminates. High pressure sodium bulbs last about twice as long as metal halide lamps but cost slightly more. They emit light strong at the red/orange end of the spectrum and promote flowering and fruiting. If your goal is lots of bloom, use high pressure sodium lamps, but remember, their light has a red/orange cast and distorts the colors of everything it illuminates.

Incandescent grow-bulbs are the least efficient means of artificial illumination. A lot of their energy is given off as

heat, rather than as visible light, and foliage can burn if placed too close to the bulb. The intensity of incandescent light is low, but can be used to supplement natural light for orchids like *Paphiopedilum* and *Phalaenopsis*.

Whether you start out by augmenting existing light or by growing orchids with no natural light whatsoever, artificial illumination allows you to flex your orchid-growing muscles and expand your plant choices. Which brings us to our next challenge.

Moisture, Moisture Everywhere

For as long as people have been growing tropical plants in temperate climates, they have struggled to give their exotic transplants the growing conditions they so richly deserve. Before central heating was the norm, growers had to worry about temperature in addition to humidity, but today we can take temperature for granted (most of the orchids recommended here grow well in normal household temperatures) and concentrate on raising the humidity around our orchids.

You may have visited a botanical garden and seen an elaborate orchid case furnished with fans and lights. Or perhaps you've seen pictures in history books of Victorian glass cases full of lush tropical ferns. Both of these setups accomplish something very important: they create a highly humid atmosphere within the enclosure of the case. You can do the same thing simply, quickly, and inexpensively.

First, check the garage, attic, or basement for an aquarium that no one is using. If you or your children never had any tropical fish, head for the nearest discount department store and buy yourself a tank. Choose one that will fit where you want to grow your orchids, perhaps on a small table in front of a bright window. Used aquariums frequently turn up at flea markets or junk shops, so keep your eyes open.

Decide how many orchid pots will fit in your aquarium. It's very important not to crowd the case. If plants are grown too close together, air won't circulate among them and the risk of disease increases greatly. A fifteen-gallon tank should comfortably hold four or five small pots, so select the specimens you think would best benefit from the rain forest climate you're about to create.

Add a layer of clean gravel to the aquarium, about 2 inches deep. Place your plants on the gravel, making sure their foliage doesn't touch the glass sides. Wet foliage can burn when the suns rays are focused on it through glass. If you'd like to vary the heights of your plants, place a few pots on top of flat rocks or overturned pots to create a "skyline effect." Add water to the bottom of your aquarium, but stop before it rises above the level of the gravel. You don't want the pots sitting in water, or their roots may rot.

I suggest you don't cover your tank. The glass walls alone will keep much of the humidity around the foliage and the overall effect will be like that of a giant drywell. Plants will need to be watered less frequently than they would if they were out in the open, and keeping the

(LEFT): Fill your terrarium with a two-inch layer of clean gravel or pebbles. (RIGHT): Place your orchids to provide adequate air circulation around the foliage.

Here's an aerial view of your planted fish tank.

tank uncovered will allow fresh air to circulate around the foliage. If you cover your aquarium, make sure you use glass or clear plastic so you don't reduce available light. Also, pay close attention to your plants, and watch for signs of disease that may thrive in stagnant air or when water condenses on the leaves.

If you're especially handy (or know someone who is) and enjoy growing orchids in your improvised case, consider building a larger setup with light tubes and fans. Because these units are self-contained, they can be placed anywhere in your home without regard to natural light. Ready-made units are also available in many sizes and finishes and are frequently advertised in the back of orchid magazines.

So, no more complaints about how you don't have the right conditions to grow orchids. With a few inexpensive items and the right plant choices, you'll be blooming in no time.

BEST PLANTS FOR AQUARIUM GARDEN

These miniature orchids are well suited to aquarium culture because of their small stature. They'll also appreciate the high humidity. (Heights listed in the table include the height of the pot.)

Orchids for Wimps	Height
Phalaenopsis (miniature species)	8"
Dendrobium (miniature species)	10"
Oncidium (miniature species)	6"
Cattleya Alliance *(miniature species)*	6-10"
Encyclia cochleata	10"
Doritis pulcherrima	10"
Cochleanthes amazonica	8"
Gongora quinquenervis	10"

In case you haven't guessed, orchid growing is contagious. The more you do, the more you want to do, and the more you want other people to do it with you. It's just a matter of time before you start enticing your friends to try an orchid or two. Maybe you give them a plantlet that's grown on one of your older plants. "Here, Libby, try this. It's easy. It's free." Before you know it, Libby is hooked.

If you're going to start trading orchids and giving them away, you've got to know how to propagate them. Propagation is a fancy word that basically means making more orchids from the ones you've already got. Professional growers frequently hybridize orchids, producing seedlings they hope will exhibit certain desirable

Phalaenopsis Red Hot Imp with seed pods.

characteristics. Orchid seed is tiny, like grains of powder, and a single ounce can contain one million seeds. Special laboratories clone orchids

Chapter 7

Propagation
and Repotting

under sterile conditions, thereby producing exact genetic replicas of prize plants more quickly than they could grow from seed.

For the home grower, however, there is a much simpler way to propagate orchids: multiplication by division. If you've ever gardened outdoors, you've probably had to dig up and divide a perennial plant that's gotten too big for its place in the border. Dividing orchids is very similar—and very simple.

Keikis

Keiki is the Hawaiian word for "baby" and refers to the small orchids that grow on other orchids. It's a simple procedure to separate these plantlets from the parent plant and pot them up on their own.

On monopodial orchids, keikis form on the central stem (like *Vandas*) or the bloom stalk (like *Phalaenopsis*). After two or three aerial roots have formed on the plantlet, carefully cut the keiki off of the stem or stalk where it's growing, using a sterile blade to cut below the roots. Trim the stem as close as possible to the young roots without damaging them. Choose a small pot, about two inches in diameter, and pour a thin layer of fine-grade orchid mix into the bottom. Center the young orchid in the pot with one hand, and fill in with orchid bark with the other, gently pushing bark pieces down among the

(LEFT): **This keiki is ready to be removed from the mother plant.**
(TOP RIGHT): **A newly potted keiki will benefit from daily misting.**
(BOTTOM RIGHT): **Note the orchid clip holding the keiki in place.**

roots. You may want to use a special orchid clip to hold the new plant in place. Soak the pot well before finding a place for it, and give your young plant extra TLC for a few weeks while it adjusts to life on its own.

Sympodial keikis can be treated in much the same way, and removing them from the parent plant is only slightly different. These keikis branch out from an existing orchid stem and send roots down toward the potting mix. When the roots get to be between one and two inches long, remove the keiki from the parent stem; you'll need to cut the keiki below the roots without damaging the roots themselves, so be careful. Once the offspring has been separated, pot it up as described above.

(ABOVE): This *Oncidium* **really needs repotting. (LEFT): The keiki on this** *Dendrobium* **has well-developed roots of it own. It's time to remove the plantlet and give it its own pot.**

Perhaps one of your orchids has outgrown its pot and needs to be transplanted. This might also be a good time to refresh a decomposed potting mix, and trim any roots, leaves, or pseudobulbs that have rotted or don't look their best. The general rule for **potting up** is to choose a pot one size larger than the pot the orchid is currently in. Pots usually come in two-inch increments, so if your orchid has outgrown a four-inch pot, you'll want to move it to a six-inch pot. The number refers to the diameter of the top of the pot.

To remove your orchid from its present pot, knock the pot against the edge of a table or countertop. Gently pull on a stem, and if the orchid doesn't budge, push up through one of the drainage holes with a wooden dowel. If your orchid still won't come out, you'll need to run a knife around the inside edge of the pot to sever any roots that are stuck to the walls of the pot.

Remove as much of the old potting mix as possible from the root system of your orchid. Gently pull the old bark out from the root mass, or rinse it away with water. While you're at it, smell the mix. Does it smell sour? If so, it was a good idea to repot. Examine the roots and trim any that are black and/or mushy. Healthy roots will be plump and white.

It's a good idea to thoroughly moisten your new potting mix before working with it, so it will be easier to handle. Add a layer of mix to the bottom of the new pot and place your orchid where you want it. For a monopodial orchid, this will be at the center of the pot. Make sure you plant your orchid at the same level it was before. That is, do not plant it deeper, covering the crown of the plant, or shallower, exposing the root system. Fill in around the roots with bark mix, gently pushing the potting medium in between the roots. Soak the orchid in its pot thoroughly, let it drain, then put the pot back in its place.

A sympodial orchid should be positioned differently when being repotted. These orchids grow across the pot in one direction, each new growth directly following the previous year's growth in a straight line. It's easy to figure out which is the growing end. If you have pseudobulbs that no longer produce leaves, that is the old end of your orchid. If you know where last year's flower came from, that is the new end. Place the old end up against the wall of the pot, leaving the growing end with space for growth. Fill in with potting medium as described above, soak, drain, and replace your orchid in its spot.

Cattleya Makeover

Sometimes an orchid just needs a little sprucing up. It may be perfectly healthy but not look its best after a tough summer outdoors. Or maybe it's a stray you've adopted, and you want to give it a makeover before you add it to your home display.

I inherited a *Cattleya* orchid from a friend who didn't know how to care for it. She'd kept it outdoors all summer, and when fall came, she knew it was time to bring the plant inside. But she also realized it looked pretty straggly and she didn't know what to do. *Cattleyas* are such good orchids for beginners, it was worth taking the

The roots of this *Cattleya* had grown so attached to the pot that the pot had to be broken in order to repot the orchid. (FACING PAGE): This made-over *Cattleya* bloomed again in less than a year.

time to give this plant a makeover and a new lease on life.

1. Notice how many pseudobulbs have lost their leaves and how many roots are growing out of the pot.

2. To remove the orchid from its pot, poke a dowel or your finger up through the hole in the bottom of the pot to loosen the plant. Or firmly bang the pot against the side of a counter or table to loosen the orchid. Then, gently tug on the pseudobulbs to pull the orchid from its pot.

3. If your orchid is severely overgrown, like the *Cattleya* in the photo, you may have to break the pot to get the plant out. In a case like this, gently detach the roots that have grown onto the sides of the pot. Don't worry if a few get left behind or are broken in the process, but do be as careful as possible.

4. Using sterilized pruning shears, cut off any pseudobulbs that no longer have leaves. Also, cut off all roots that look stringy or brown and rotten. Since you're removing some of the plant's top growth it's okay to prune the roots as well. Less foliage means the plant needs less root mass to support it.

5. Using your fingers, gently remove as much of the old potting medium as possible from the root ball.

6. Choose a new pot for your orchid. If you've trimmed a lot of roots, you may need a pot one size (two inches in diameter) smaller than the pot it came out of. You want the orchid to have room to grow, but you don't want it to be dwarfed by its pot.

7. Cover the holes in the bottom of your new pot with pieces of broken pottery or landscape cloth. Add a layer of potting mix to the bottom of the pot, then place your trimmed and groomed orchid inside, remembering to place the older growths against the wall of the pot.

8. Holding the orchid with one hand, add bark chips around the orchid with the other, gently firming the orchid in place as you go.

9. Note the proportion of the plant to pot. The aesthetic should be right and give the plant room to grow for a year or two.

10. Soak the entire pot in a bowl or saucepan for 15 minutes, then let it drain in the sink. This thoroughly wets the new potting medium.

11. Place your newly made-over orchid in a spot out of the sun for the next 10-14 days, while it recovers from the shock of surgery. In two weeks, give it a sunny spot and watch for signs of new growth. This probably won't be until early spring, so be patient. It will be worth the wait.

Planting an Orchid Box

If your orchid came in a pot and you'd like to try moving it to an orchid box, here's how:

1. *Gently remove your orchid from its pot and shake off as much of the potting mix as possible, to free the roots.*

2. *Line your wooden box with a piece of sheet moss. Bags of sheet moss are available at home improvement centers and plant stores, and contain several flat sheets of dried moss. This will keep the potting medium from washing out through the slats.*

(LEFT): **The potted *Oncidium* is a good choice for a slatted orchid box.** (RIGHT): **Soak your orchid box after planting.**

Chapter 8

Special
Projects

3. Sprinkle a thin layer of bark mix over the bottom of the box.

4. Place your orchid gently in the center of the box.

5. While holding your orchid in place with one hand, pour small amounts of bark mix around the edges, gently poking it under and around the roots until the orchid can stand on its own.

6. Finish filling the box with bark mix, to just below the edge of the top slat.

7. Soak your planted orchid box in a shallow bowl for 10-15 minutes so the potting medium gets thoroughly wet, then let it drain in the sink.

Building an Orchid Tree

Perhaps you're feeling so confident now, with your newly acquired orchid-growing skills, that you'd like to try something a little different, a little artistic. How about planting an orchid tree?

Many of the orchids described in this book are epiphytes, i.e., in nature they grow on other plants. Their roots hold them in place on a branch or trunk, as well as absorb water and nutrients. An orchid tree gives you lots of vertical growing space without taking up much room at your window, and it can provide epiphytic orchids with the excellent root aeration so many of them require.

Epiphytic orchids can easily be mounted on branches to mimic the way they grow in nature. If you have creative flair, planting an orchid tree is a chance to create a thing of rare and unique beauty. You will feel an enormous sense of accomplishment when you're done.

Start with some of the tougher orchids that will thrive, take root, and prosper in a home environment. Many of the more drought-tolerant orchids can be recognized by their thick, waxy foliage. These include *Phalaenopsis, Doritis, Brassavola, Cattleya* (and members of the *Cattleya* Alliance), and *Dendrobium*. You might also try *Ascocentrum*, which resemble *Vanda* orchids but are quite a bit smaller.

Don't go overboard when choosing your plants; your orchid tree will look better if you limit yourself to three or four different orchids. You don't want them compet-

This *Phalaenopsis* is an excellent candidate for an orchid tree. It's been taken out of its pot and is ready to be mounted.

Every orchid tree is unique.

ing with each other for attention. Rather, they should work together as a cohesive whole.

First, choose your branch or log. You should have an idea of where you want to put your finished orchid tree, so you can choose a branch of the appropriate size. Look for one with an interesting shape, a branching habit that suits you, and perhaps some nooks and crannies where you can tuck a small specimen. Look at your branch from every angle. Trim any unwanted twigs, and if your branch is dirty or covered with lichen, scrub it with a 10% bleach solution and let it dry.

Do you want your orchid branch to hang or to be free-standing? Each approach has advantages:

A hanging branch looks quite dramatic across a large window or wall. Use stainless steel eyes to screw into the back or top of the branch, then apply a dab of glue to cement each one in place. These eyes can be hung from hooks screwed into your window frame, or strung with a thin cable. Be sure to consider the weight of your branch when deciding how many hooks and eyes to use and when choosing a cable.

POINTS TO REMEMBER FOR WORKING WITH ORCHIDS NOT IN SOIL

1. Remember, orchid roots dry out more quickly when they're exposed to the air than when they're surrounded by soil.

2. Soak your orchid's roots in a bowl for five minutes before working with them; they'll be more pliable, less fragile, and easier to work with.

3. Hot glue should only be used on plant tissue at the "low" setting. The "high" setting on a hot glue gun can burn and kill plant tissue.

4. When tying orchids to wood, bark, or fern fibre, make sure to wrap the orchid roots in sphagnum moss. Otherwise the wire or fishing line used to tie the orchid in place may cut into the plant tissue. The sphagnum moss will also help keep the orchid's roots moist.

5. Make it easy to spritz your mounted orchid. By having a spray bottle on hand, you can mist its roots whenever you're passing by.

6. Mounted orchids will require regular foliar feeding, so keep a mister with a half-strength solution of fertilizer convenient.

A free-standing tree can easily be moved from place to place, should you want to rearrange your interior landscape, and it may be easier to assemble, since you can approach it from all angles. A clay pot makes an excellent base. The weight of the pot helps keep the branch upright, and the terra cotta blends in well with the rest of your potted plants. Position the branch in the pot and add stones around the base of the branch for ballast. Make sure the drainage hole of the pot is covered, and, wearing gloves, pour quikrete or plaster of Paris into the pot, firming it in around the base of your branch. Even though the surface of each of these materials dries in 20-30 minutes, let it dry overnight before you start work.

While the plaster dries, think about possible orchid arrangements. The more time you spend on this, the less time you'll waste fumbling with plant material when it is most vulnerable, with its roots exposed to the air. When you are happy with your composition, assemble the rest of your tools.

A drop cloth is a must for easy clean-up. You'll also need sphagnum moss, transparent fishing line, and/or thin gauge wire. Your plants will be attached to the tree with five-pound test monofilament or wire, and sphagnum moss. Remove the first plant from its pot, shaking off as

much potting mix as possible. Don't be afraid to comb through the roots with your fingers. These plants can take a little manhandling.

Wrap the root system in moss and tie the moss/root bundle to the tree. Wire may be easier to work with, but fishing line is almost invisible. If your branch has small side twigs, you may be able to tuck the moss/root bundle into a natural niche without any tying whatsoever. After about six months, you should be able to remove the wire or line; the roots of the orchid will have grown onto the branch.

Choose the focal point of your branch and start there, working outward. Begin with your largest orchid, so that smaller plants can be used to fill in gaps. Pause as you work, and look at your orchid tree from every angle, being sure not to overplant. This is a case where less is more; plant too many orchids and no single plant will shine.

Congratulations, your tree is planted. Because these orchids are not growing in soil (which retains water and nutrients), they'll require more frequent attention, much as slab-mounted orchids do. Obviously, they can't be watered in the traditional manner, so consider an alternate method of watering or misting. Orchid branches can be brought to the sink or tub for soaking. A free-standing epiphyte tree can stand under the shower. Don't forget to allow the branch to drip dry before returning it to its place.

You should water your orchid tree twice a week, but in an emergency, it's possible to get it through a one week absence. Place your branch in the shower and open the faucet so that the smallest possible trickle of lukewarm water drips to the floor. (Make sure the drain is open.) Close the shower curtain and reduce the light to a minimum. With little light, the orchids' need for water is reduced and the increased humidity of the closed dripping shower will suffice.

What you'll need:

1. branch

2. terra cotta pot

3. ballast stones

4. plaster of Paris or quikrete

5. drop cloth

6. epiphytic orchids

7. long-grain sphagnum moss

8. five-pound test monofilament or thin-gauge wire

Epidendrum **Hokulea**

Pests

There comes a time in every orchid grower's life when she or he looks at a beloved plant, does a double take, and says, "Oh, no, what is that?" Occasionally orchids are attacked by insect pests or diseases that can do quite a bit of damage if left unchecked. In general, orchids are fairly pest-free plants, so there's no reason to expect trouble. But since you want to succeed with orchids, why not arm yourself with the necessary know-how? The descriptions in this chapter should help you identify a potential problem.

A few sound cultural practices will keep the spread of insects and disease at a minimum:

1. *Whenever you introduce a new orchid into your home, isolate it for a week or two and watch carefully. When you're sure it's disease- and pest-free, integrate the plant into your collection.*

Chapter 9

Pests and
Diseases

2. Keep your growing areas neat. Debris can be a breeding ground for both insects and disease, so clean up dead leaves and flowers as they fall.

3. Pay attention to the individual needs of your plant: temperature, light, food, and water. Just as we humans are better able to fight off a cold when we're strong and well-nourished, orchids are better able to fight off infection when they're well-grown and properly watered and fed.

4. Early detection is key to keeping your orchids healthy. Check your plant when you first receive it or when you're choosing it in the store. If you see anything that looks like an insect pest, don't buy it. And look closely at your plants each time you water, so you'll notice any unwanted "diners" before they have a chance to get established.

Some people are reluctant to use chemicals in their home because of their toxicity. It's always wise to start with the least toxic method available, and if it works, great. If not, you can either step up the attack, or get rid of the plant and start fresh. If you have children or pets and you feel uncomfortable about keeping insecticides in the house, then don't do it. Many problems can be eliminated by consistent care and regular application of harmless household ingredients. If you don't mind keeping a few insecticides around, several on the market are suitable for in-home use and are very effective.

There are jagged holes in my orchid's leaves! What's eating them?
It's probably a slug. Check for silvery trails that both snails and slugs can leave behind on plant leaves. While slugs aren't usually household pests, they can easily be brought inside on plant material when they are small and difficult to see. However, the damage they cause is anything but.

Slugs like a warm, moist environment, just as your orchids do, and your home is a safe haven for them, without natural predators like birds or toads. Slugs are nocturnal creatures, so you won't always catch them in the act, but you can lure them into oblivion with some well-positioned saucers of slug-dissolving beer. (It's one of the few things they find tastier than *Phalaenopsis* leaves.) Place a few among your orchids and wait. Slugs will find the beer, climb into the saucers to drink, and be dissolved by the liquid. Check your beer traps every morning and replenish them as needed. After a few weeks, you should be able to stop putting out bait.

There are white cottony dots in the nooks and crannies of my orchid. Is this something I should worry about?
Yup. This is mealybug, scourge of the tropical plant world. Okay, one of the scourges of the tropical plant world. Fortunately, it's easy to spot, thanks to the insect's waxy, white covering. Unfortunately, this covering is highly protective and many sprays cannot penetrate it.

(TOP LEFT, RIGHT): Slug damage on *Phalaenopsis* leaves (BOTTOM LEFT): Slug damage on a *Phalaenopsis* flower

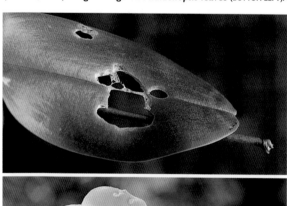

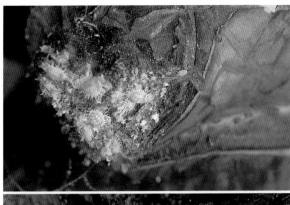

Mealybugs look like dots of cotton.

Mealybugs are sucking insects. They attach themselves to the leaves of your plants with their **proboscis** and suck the plant juices out of the foliage. By removing the insects, you kill them (since the proboscis is left behind in the leaf), so you don't have to worry about mealybugs latching onto another plant if they fall out of your grasp. Mature mealybugs don't move around and can be wiped off your plant with a Q-tip dipped in rubbing alcohol. The alcohol dissolves their protective waxy coat and kills them.

Immature mealybugs can and do move around, so plan a twofold attack. (You need to eliminate all stages of mealybugs or the reproductive cycle will continue.) First, spray foliage with a 10% solution of rubbing alcohol, i.e., nine parts water to one part alcohol. Repeat after ten days. Then, collect a few used cigarette butts. Peel the paper off the filters and poke them in the potting mix. The nicotine absorbed by the cigarette's filter is an effective insecticide.

If these home remedies don't eliminate your mealybugs, try an oil-based spray in combination with a **systemic granule**. The oil will dissolve the waxy covering the mealybugs have, and the granule will be absorbed by the plant, making it, in essence, poisonous to the insects feeding on it. Make sure that any insecticide you purchase is specifically labeled as effective against the insect you have, and follow the instructions on the label regarding frequency of application.

There are ants on my plants. Is this a problem?
Not in and of itself, but ants frequently act as shepherds to herds of mealybugs, aphids, and other insects. (Strange but true.) So, if you see ants on a regular basis, look for an insect infestation. Another sign that you may have a problem is a sticky liquid on the leaves of your plants. This is called **honeydew** and is excreted by sucking insects. Finally, a powdery black film on the foliage (**sooty mold**) sometimes grows in honeydew, and may also indicate the presence of an insect population.

I see small brown dots on the leaves of my orchid. They don't move and I can scrape them off with my fingernail. What are they?
Believe it or not, these are also insects. They're called scale and they're related to mealybugs except instead of a waxy, white protective coating they have a hard, brown protective coating, which is even more effective. As with the mealybug, removing scale from the plant kills the insect. The same methods that are effective against mealybugs will work on scale.

When I'm misting my orchids I notice small webs in the leaf axils. I can't see them most of the time. What is this?
This is spider mite webbing. Spider mites are particularly insidious pests, because they are very small and hard to detect. Frequently, you'll notice the damage to the plant before you detect the spider mite itself. If you notice a leaf looks yellow and speckled, check for spider mites. If you notice that the plant looks dull and has no sheen, check for spider mites. And if you see webbing when you mist your plant, check for spider mites.

Scale insects don't look like insects at all.

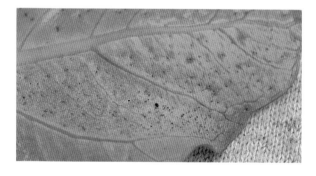

(TOP AND MIDDLE): **Spider mite webbing is easier to detect than the insects themselves.** (BOTTOM): **These spider mites look like tiny red dots on the back of this leaf.**

To check for spider mites, look at the underside of a leaf with a magnifying glass. If you see tiny red or white eight-legged creatures moving around, you've got spider mites. If you don't have a magnifying glass but you can see little dots with your naked eye, poke one. If it moves, you've got spider mites. Or, tap on the top of the leaf while holding it over a piece of white paper. If small dots fall onto the paper, you've got spider mites.

Spider mites are sucking pests, and they are highly mobile. (Check surrounding plants to see if they have spread. You may want to spray a little water onto the leaves of neighboring plants to help you detect any webbing.) First, remove any foliage that is substantially damaged, and dispose of the infested leaves. Spider mites can be killed with a solution of soap and cold water sprayed onto foliage with a mister. Or, put a little dishwashing liquid on your hands, rub it up and down the front and back of your orchid's foliage and let it sit a while. After 15-20 minutes, rinse the soap off the foliage thoroughly. Repeat this at three-day intervals in the summer and five-day intervals in

the winter, until you see no more sign of spider mites.

A combination of systemic granule and liquid spray is also effective against spider mites. You can choose a pyrethrin-based spray, which is not toxic to humans, or an oil-based spray. Once you've got the problem under control, consider preventive medicine: a rinse with soapy, cold water once every two or three weeks should keep spider mites from gaining control.

There are aphids on my orchid bud. I've waited so long for this plant to flower and now I'm afraid I'll lose the bloom. What do I do?
Aphids don't usually attack orchids, but sometimes the flower buds are attractive to this insect. The problem is, if you spray a bud with an insecticide, you will probably lose the flower. While this is certainly preferable to losing the entire plant, first try removing the aphids by hand. Gently wipe the aphids off the bud with a wet paper towel and repeat as needed. You may save your flower. If the problem persists, spray the orchid when its bloom is finished.

Diseases

Diseases are somewhat more difficult to diagnose, but fortunately, they are also pretty rare. Be sure to start with healthy plants and provide them with good growing conditions; a strong, well-grown plant is better able to resist infection. As with insect pests, early detection is the key to controlling plant disease.

The leaves of my plant are covered with black (or brown) mushy spots that start out small and get bigger, until the whole leaf is black. This can't be good.
You are so right. Orchids are susceptible to several different kinds of fungal and bacterial diseases and many of them look a lot alike.

Most plant diseases are caused by fungus, and there's an easy way to tell if this is your problem. Cut off a piece of leaf with black spots, mist it, and seal it in a resealable plastic bag. This creates a moist chamber for incubation. Put the bag someplace out of the way, and let it sit. After a week, take the leaf out of the bag and look at it with a magnifying glass. Do you see fungus growing on the leaves? If so, your plant has a fungal disease.

Fungus thrives in cool, wet conditions, so try not to allow water to stand on your orchid's foliage or flowers. If you water early in the day, any splashes of water should have time to dry before cooler evening temperatures provide the perfect breeding ground for fungus.

This *Phalaenopsis* shows signs of fungal damage.

If your plant is severely damaged, throw it away. This is no time to be sentimental; a diseased orchid may lead to infection of neighboring plants. If only a few leaves have been damaged, cut them off with a sterilized blade or scissors. Then, spray or dust the cut with a fungicide formulated for orchids. If you need a fungicide fast and don't have one on hand, sprinkle the leaves of your orchid with cinnamon. It may look funny but it smells good, and cinnamon is an excellent fungicide.

Okay, I tried that thing with the resealable plastic bag but no fungus grew.
Maybe your plant has a bacterial disease. Fortunately, many of the remedies are the same. First, decide if your plant is worth saving. If so, cut off any damaged leaves and spray with Physan or another antibacterial spray suitable for orchids. It's always best to spray outside if possible, but if your orchid gets sick in winter and you live in New Hampshire, you're obviously not going to bring your *Phalaenopsis* outdoors to spray. In this case, bring your plant to the garage or cellar, or lay a plastic tarp down on the floor before you spray to keep drips off your floor and furniture.

Why do I have to cut with sterilized scissors? Isn't washing them good enough?
No. Bacteria, fungi, and viruses enter plants through wounds, and washing the blade of your knife or scissors won't get rid of all the microscopic organisms. Therefore, always be careful when pruning your plants and sterilize the blade before moving on to the next orchid. This can be done by rinsing your blade in alcohol, holding your scissors over a flame, or baking them for an hour at 300°F.

What does a plant virus look like?
The virus itself is microscopic and attacks the plant on a cellular level. If the leaves of your orchid look streaked or mottled, or have concentric black rings on them, this may be a sign of a virus. However, a plant can look perfectly healthy and still be infected. There is no cure for plant viruses and they can only be confirmed by laboratory testing. If you suspect you have an infected plant, throw it away. Most reputable growers test for viruses periodically, and as a result, viral diseases are not widespread among orchids. Buy your plants from growers you can trust or who give you a guarantee. If you have an infected plant, get rid of it and the potting medium it was planted in. The pot itself may be reused after being soaked for at least an hour in a solution of one cup bleach in one gallon of water.

Please don't let all this information scare you off. I want you to be well-armed with knowledge, to know what you're looking for. But the fact is, orchids are relatively pest- and disease-free. If you pay attention to the cultural requirements of your plants and keep an eye out for bugs when you water, you may never have a problem.

PEST AND DISEASE I.D.

If the leaves of your orchid are covered with a sticky substance (honeydew) or a black powdery substance (**sooty mold**), this may signal the presence of one of the pests listed below, such as mealybug or scale.

Pest/Disease	Damage
Slugs	silvery trails on and around plants; jagged holes in leaves
Mealybugs	white, cottony masses in the leaf axils and along leaves and stems
Ants	ants crawling on a plant usually signify that an insect such as scale or mealybug is present
Scale	hard, brown dots, the size of a pin-head, along leaves and stems
Spider mites	fine webbing in the leaf axils and leaves; mottled, yellowish coloring of foliage
Aphids	small insects (in several colors) concentrate their feeding on the sugary flower buds
Fungal diseases	black mushy spots on leaves; test in a moist chamber for presence of fungus
Bacterial diseases	black spots on leaves; no fungus grows in a moist chamber
Viral diseases	black rings on leaves; foliage streaked, mottled, or discolored

1. My orchid seems healthy, it's got new leaves but it's not blooming. What's wrong?

Maybe nothing. Every orchid has its own bloom cycle, and once you know what it is, you'll know when to expect your plant to bloom.

For example, Phalaenopsis orchids bloom once a year, and the flowers can last for months. If you got your orchid in bloom in January and it stopped blooming in April, you can expect to see a new spike starting the following November or December for January bloom. In the meantime, your Phal will put out two or three new leaves if it's happy, so keep your eye on the foliage growth and color. If the plant is growing and the leaves are a good medium green, be patient. Your orchid will probably bloom again.

2. The leaves of my orchid are turning yellow. Do I need to feed it?

Not necessarily. Yellow leaves can mean a few different things.

Chapter 10

Frequently Asked

Questions

(TOP): **This rotten pseudobulb should be surgically removed.** (BOTTOM): **The original bloom stalk of this Phal was broken just above the open flower, and a new spike sprouted from the node below.**

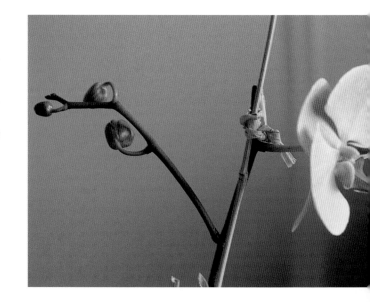

- If your orchid is getting too much light, the foliage may look yellowish. Check the orchid profiles in Chapter Four and adjust the placement of your plant, if indicated.

- The early stages of overwatering may also be signaled by yellowing foliage. If your orchid likes to dry out between waterings, make sure you don't overwater, or your orchid may rot and die.

- Finally, yellow leaves can be a sign of a nitrogen deficiency. You may need to increase the frequency of your feeding, but never increase the concentration of the fertilizer beyond that suggested on the plant food container. An application that is too strong can burn the roots and kill a plant. If you are already feeding your orchid with a balanced fertilizer every two weeks at full strength, you might try switching to a food with a higher concentration of nitrogen, i.e., with a higher first number.

3. There are roots growing up into the air instead of down into the soil. Should I bury them?

No. By now you're familiar with the term epiphyte, meaning a plant that in nature grows perched in a tree. The word comes from the Greek, "epi" meaning on, and "phyte" meaning plant. Epiphytes are not parasites and take no nutrition from the host plant; the tree is simply a place to live. Epiphytes have special roots covered with a super-absorbent material called velamen. These velamen roots anchor the epiphytic orchid to its host and quickly absorb moisture and nutrients from the atmosphere and seasonal rains. Velamen roots frequently grow in several directions, since one of their functions is to anchor the plants in place, and the more extensive the network of roots, the more securely anchored the orchid. The roots you see growing up into the air are just looking for a place to anchor. Be aware that this is their natural growth habit and these roots do not want to be buried. If you don't like the look, consider growing a different kind of orchid or moving your current orchid to a bark or wood mount.

4. The pseudobulb is mushy and smells bad. What should I do?

Minimize your losses. Mushy is never good, and the bad smell tells you something is rotting on your windowsill. If you've caught the problem early enough, you may be able to save your plant. Usually you should wait to repot your orchid until after it has bloomed, but if there's rot involved, knock it out of its pot ASAP. Examine the roots and if any are rotten, trim them off with sterilized scissors. Next, determine the extent of the mushiness. Each bulb with even a little rot must be removed. Sterilize the blade of a large, sharp knife and slice off the rotting pseudobulbs. Try to cut between the bulbs and down through the roots, then pull apart the rotted areas from the firm growth. Check the healthy parts of the plant for open wounds that you may have inadvertently caused. If you find any, dust them with a fungicide. (Sulfur powder is available at many pharmacies and is an effective fungicidal powder.) Repot the healthy portion of your orchid (probably in a smaller pot), and put it in a spot out of direct sun to let it recuperate, for about two weeks. Since overwatering may have been the cause of this problem, be sure to adjust your watering schedule.

5. My five-year-old broke the bloom stalk of my **Phalaenopsis** *before the flowers finished blooming. Can I save the bloom?*

There's a good chance you can. *Phalaenopsis* orchids are one species of orchid that reliably rebloom from their original spike. If the flower stalk is broken at the very

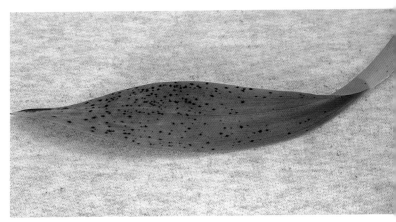

These black spots are typical of water damage; they are *not* fatal.

base of the plant it probably won't rebloom. Cut off the jagged stalk and feed it with a bloom booster to encourage another spike to grow. If you don't see signs of a spike within two months, you'll probably have to wait a year. (Remember, Phals usually only bloom once a year.) If the stalk has been broken farther up the stem, you may be in luck. Cut the stem just above the last remaining node, and care for your orchid as usual. About 60% of the time a Phal will send out another bloom spike from the stem node, and you should have flowers within six to eight weeks.

6. There are black spots all over the leaves of my orchid. Should I cut them off?

Perhaps, but we need a little more information first. How big are the spots and are they spreading? Many orchids, especially *Oncidiums*, get black spots on their leaves from cold-water damage to leaf tissue. These spots are usually small and do not spread. Most orchids can live with a certain amount of this, although aesthetically they are undesirable. If the black spots start out small, but turn large and mushy, spreading across the foliage and pseudobulbs, then get out the knife. This is probably a fungal infection and can kill an orchid if not caught in time. Sterilize a pair of scissors and cut off the spotted part of the leaves. Then, spray with a fungicide specifically intended for orchids, or dust the cut edge with a sprinkling of cinnamon. If the black spots have spread to the pseudobulbs, treat them as in question #4 above and remove the infected plant parts.

7. Should I cut the bloom stalk after my orchid has finished flowering? Where?

Yes. Where, depends on what kind of orchid you have. Most orchids will not rebloom from the same stalk, so

the spike should be cut off as close to the base of the plant as possible. If you have a *Phalaenopsis* you may get the orchid to rebloom from its original flower spike. When the flowers have died back, cut the stalk between the lowest flower and the node just below it. Care for your Phal as usual and watch for a bloom spike within six to eight weeks. If you've decided to try growing a *Psychopsis*, leave the entire bloom stalk in place. As long as it stays green there's a chance you may get more flowers from the same stalk. If it dries out and turns brown, cut the stalk off as close to the base of the plant as possible.

8. The leaves of my orchid look leathery and wrinkled. What's wrong?

You're orchid isn't getting enough water, and before you can solve the problem, you have to figure out why. A wrinkled leaf is a sign of dehydration, and dehydration can be the result of infrequent watering, or, interestingly enough, of overwatering. Knock your orchid out of its pot and look at the roots. If they are white and look healthy and the potting mix doesn't smell bad, underwatering may be the culprit. Check the recommended watering schedule in the individual orchid profile section of this book and adjust accordingly. If you've been watering your orchid once every seven days, try watering once every six days for the next three weeks and mist the leaves daily. If the leaves still look wrinkled, try watering every five days for another three weeks and watch for improvement.

If the roots of your orchid appear brown and rotten and if the potting mix smells unpleasant, overwatering may be the culprit. When an orchid is watered too frequently, its roots can rot as a result, and the plant can no longer absorb necessary water and nutrients. Trim the rotted roots. If there are any healthy roots remaining, repot your orchid and adjust your watering schedule. Put your plant on a drywell and mist the leaves daily. This will supplement the reduced amount of water that the damaged root system can deliver.

9. My orchid had a full stalk of flower buds, and one day they all fell off. Why did this happen?

This is called **blasting**, and it usually happens because the temperature is too low or the plant is too dry. An orchid with maturing flowers is at a very vulnerable stage and requires a little bit of special attention. When the flowers are in bud, it's particularly important to keep them out of drafts. If you usually keep your orchid in a window so that it can benefit from a nighttime temperature drop, move it farther into the room when buds form. When the plant has finished flowering you can safely move it back to its original spot. Also, when an orchid is in bud, it should not be allowed to dry out thoroughly between waterings, even if it is a drought-tolerant epiphyte. Don't go overboard, simply increase the frequency of your watering by a day or two, depending on the season. If you mist your orchid, be sure not to mist the buds themselves.

10. How do I know when it's time to repot?

There are several signs to look for. First of all, consider how long the orchid has been in the same potting mix. Some orchids like to be repotted every year. No orchid should stay in mix that's more than three years old. If your orchid has been in the same pot and mix for three years, you should definitely repot. If it's been less than three years, look carefully at the consistency of the mix. Are the bark pieces smaller than they were originally? Does the mix smell funny? If so, you should probably repot. If not, check again in another six months.

Second, don't repot when your orchid is in bloom or spike. No matter how good you are at repotting, there's bound to be a little trauma to the roots, and you run the risk of losing your flowers. If your orchid is in spike, wait until it's finished flowering before you repot. If you suspect your orchid is about to put out a spike (because you have a Phal, it's January, and your Phal always blooms in January) go ahead and wait for your flower, then repot.

Finally, if your orchid is outgrowing its pot (e.g., it's getting huge, the pot is tipping over, the roots are growing all over the edges), you should move the orchid to a bigger pot.

Vanda **Gordon Dillon x Kapiolea**

Admit it, you're hooked. And you don't feel the slightest bit wimpy, do you? Your only problem now is that you want more orchids, more orchid-growing paraphernalia, and you'd really like someone to talk to about how wonderful orchids are and how your life would be a barren landscape without them. It's time to join a club.

Orchid societies are excellent organizations for orchid growers at any level of expertise. Membership might even include a monthly magazine subscription, a book on orchid care, a comprehensive directory of orchid growers around the world, and a discount on anything you buy from the society. Some societies even sell books, artwork, calendars, and other orchid-related material.

Orchid magazines put out by orchid societies often contain excellent photographs and articles on different orchid species and hybrids. They

Chapter 11

What's Next?

Ascocenda Suksamran 'Sunshine'

answer questions that may well be relevant to you. Advertising sections can be very helpful, especially if they include all kinds of orchid supplies as well as plants. Many regional orchid shows and events are frequently also listed.

Regional orchid clubs are also helpful and usually meet once a month. Attending meetings of a regional orchid club is a great way to meet fellow enthusiasts in your area, and learn more about who's growing what in conditions similar to yours. Most meetings include a swap table, where people trade duplicates and keikis, and members are encouraged to bring in and show off whatever they've got in flower. Regional clubs usually publish a newsletter on a regular basis.

Orchid shows can be mind-boggling, full of elaborate displays and well-stocked sales areas. The exhibits frequently include re-creations of tropical microclimates featuring unusual exotics most of us would be hard-pressed to grow at home. Still, it's fascinating to look at, and everybody likes to dream. But it's in the sales area that the fun really starts.

It's a win-win situation: orchid growers selling orchids to orchid lovers who came to buy orchids. What could be better? You know you're really in trouble when you start planning your vacations around orchid shows. I'll never forget the trip I made to the Honolulu orchid show. I traveled light, saving plenty of room in my suitcases to take home the many orchids I expected to buy at the show. If I hadn't had to worry about carrying everything home on the plane, undoubtedly I would have bought twice as much.

While many of the larger shows attract growers from all over the world, shows in tropical venues like Hawaii and Florida also include numerous local growers. Plus, you can always visit some of the nurseries when the show is over. Orchid shows in more temperate climates offer a total escape from reality. When you're surrounded by the lush warmth of the New York orchid show in the middle of February, it's easy to forget there's a big, bad, slushy city outside.

Maybe you'd prefer to buy your orchids closer to home. These days, orchids are more popular and more affordable than ever, and it's not unusual to find a large variety of plants available at your local home improvement store. As you get to know the plant department, ask the manager which day they usually receive their shipments, and try to look at the orchids when they're fresh off the

truck. I've been astonished by some of the inexpensive rarities I've found this way.

Try to buy your orchids in bud, at first. That way, you won't have to wait long for them to bloom, and the gratification of successful flowering is a great confidence builder. Look at the buds carefully before you buy. If they look yellowish or dry, stop. These buds have blasted, perhaps as a result of getting too dry or cold during shipping. Or use the situation to your advantage. Many stores will sell you damaged plants at a discount if you ask. I once got two *Dendrobiums* for the price of one because the bloom spikes had been broken.

Botanical garden gift shops and small plant shops are also good places to shop for orchids. People who love plants are almost always glad to meet someone who shares their enthusiasm, so don't be afraid to ask lots of questions before buying. A knowledgeable salesperson will be happy to make recommendations and give you complete cultural instructions.

If you live someplace devoid of plant shops, botanical gardens, and home improvement stores, there's always mail order. With internet access you can surf the web to your heart's content, searching by genus and species, by geographical region, or just by browsing through page after page of general orchid listings. Many orchid websites provide excellent photographs and cultural information as well as price lists. Remember, if you want orchids shipped to you, you'll have to wait until the temperatures in your area are appropriately warm. Just because the orchids are in bloom in their growing region doesn't mean they'll survive an overnight truck stop in a cold climate.

Catalog shopping is a good alternative for those of you without web access. Some growers charge for their catalogs, but don't be put off by this. These are frequently glossy magazines with expensive, full-color photography, and lots of growing tips and suggestions. Many growers will credit the cost of the catalog toward your first order.

It's worth the extra cost to pay for the fastest shipping available. Most orchids can survive one to three days in transit, but longer than this would be stressful for the plants. Professional growers are usually very accomplished at packing and shipping, and can successfully send orchids in bud and in bloom without any flowers dropping off. After all the anticipation that goes with placing an order, give your orchid every opportunity to arrive safely by speeding up the trip.

Glossary

aeration the exposing of a substance or object to the air

balanced fertilizer a fertilizer containing equal parts nitrogen, phosphorus, and potassium; good for overall growth of foliage, flowers, and roots

bark chips pieces of bark, frequently pine, used as a component in potting medium for epiphytic orchids

blasted blooms are said to have blasted if they have gotten too dry or cold in their formative stage and have therefore died

bloom booster a fertilizer containing more phosphorus than nitrogen or potassium; used to encourage bloom

cachepot a decorative pot, bowl, or vase into which an unattractive plant container may be placed

canopy the foliage layer of a forest, where many epiphytes live

cork the spongy, absorbent layer of bark from the cork tree (*Phellodendron amurense*); frequently used as an orchid mount

crown the central part of the leaves, from which new growth arises

cultivar a specific plant grown from seed; its name is set off by single quotation marks

cultural pertaining to the growing conditions best suited to a particular plant; light, humidity, and fertilization are all cultural requirements

cuticle the thick, waxy, protective covering secreted by leaves that reduces the rate of water loss through transpiration

division a method of propagating plants by cutting apart the pseudobulbs at the rhizome

drywell a saucer or pan of pebbles and water, which raises the ambient humidity around the plants that sit upon it

epiphyte a plant that grows above the ground attached to a branch or tree trunk; it derives no nutrients from its host but absorbs them from rain and debris

flush to water thoroughly for an extended period of time to wash any accumulated fertilizers from the potting mix

foliar feed a method of feeding accomplished by spraying a mixture of fertilizer and water onto plant leaves with a spray bottle

genera plural of genus

genus a group of orchids classified together due to common ancestry; can be manmade or naturally occurring

honeydew a sugary substance excreted by sucking insects as they feed on plant juices

horticultural charcoal a grade of charcoal used in potting mixes to absorb and deactivate acids and fungi

humus decomposing organic matter

hybrid offspring resulting from crossing two different species

intergeneric a hybrid between species of different genera

keiki a plantlet that develops on an orchid's cane or flower stalk

leaf axil the angle formed by the leaf and stem

lip a modified petal which has evolved to attract pollinators; it also acts as a landing platform for insects during pollination

microclimate a climate created in a small area to suit specific plant needs such as elevated humidity or lowered temperatures

monopodial form of orchid growth where a single shoot grows upward, e.g., *Phalaenopsis*

node joint on a bloom stalk or stem from which another stem, leaves, or roots may emerge

osmunda fiber a potting medium composed of small pieces of the dried roots of the osmunda fern

peat moss finely chopped, decomposed organic matter; usually about 75% sphagnum moss

perlite a lightweight volcanic rock that is crushed then heat-treated to make it expand; used as a potting medium

petals inner parts of a flower; petals on an orchid may resemble sepals

pine bark nuggets a potting medium composed of small pieces of pine bark

potting up repotting an orchid into a bigger pot

proboscis the beaklike mouthpart of an insect

propagate to make more plants from existing plants

pseudobulb thickened stem of a sympodial orchid that stores water

rhizome a root-bearing stem that grows horizontally across the potting mix and from which pseudobulbs arise

rootbound a plant whose root system has grown too large for its pot is considered rootbound

sepals outer parts of a flower; sepals on orchids may look similar to petals

soilless mix a potting mix composed of any of several substances, both organic and inorganic, but not including soil

sooty mold a black fungus that frequently grows in honeydew

species a further division of a genus; a closely related group of plants

sphagnum moss a bog moss used in potting media to retain moisture

sympodial form of orchid growth where new growth arises from the rhizome of the previous growth

systemic granule a granule form of a pesticide or fungicide that is absorbed by the plant, and works from inside the plant's tissues

tepals when sepals and petals are indistinguishable from each other they are called tepals

terrestrials orchids that grow on the ground

transpiration loss of water in vapor form; it takes place through a plant's foliage

tree fern fiber a potting medium composed of small pieces of the fibrous trunk of the tropical tree fern

understory the lower levels of the forest canopy that are protected from direct sun by the topmost branches

variegated multicolored

velamen a thick layer of spongelike material that covers the roots of epiphytic orchids and quickly absorbs water and nutrients

Index

About the Author

Ellen Zachos was born and raised in New Hampshire where she'd do anything to avoid yard work. Now, her company Acme Plant Stuff designs, installs, and maintains commercial and residential interior and exterior gardens in New York City.

Ellen is a Harvard graduate, a horticulturist certified at the New York Botanical Garden, a garden writer, and photographer. She lectures at the New York Botanical Garden, the Horticultural Society of New York, and at garden events across the country. She is also a regular contributor to the Brooklyn Botanic Garden's handbook series.